Best Wishes
To John,
David Thompson

ROCKY MOUNTAIN BASKETBALL

NAISMITH TO NINETEEN-NINETY

The Denver Safeways watch as coach Ev Shelton holds the ball for James Naismith, inventor of basketball, at the 1938-39 AAU finals in Denver. Photo courtesy of Dick Wells.

1985 NCAA West Regional Tournament action at Denver's McNichols Sports Arena. Photo courtesy of Rich Clarkson/ Sports Illustrated.

***Rich Clarkson**, the former director of photography of* National Geographic, *publishes photographic books and organizes photographic exhibitions from his Denver base.*

He is known for the newspaper photography staffs he developed in Topeka, Kansas, and at The Denver Post, *where he was an assistant managing editor. Clarkson has been president of the National Press Photographers Association and has long been affiliated with* Sports Illustrated, *where he is now a contract contributing photographer.*

C O N T E N T S

The warmth of the morning sun is welcome on a winter day in the Wet Mountain Valley. Photo courtesy of John Fielder, from Colorado, Images of the Alpine Landscape.

John Fielder has been photographing the natural world since 1973. He is the photographer of 10 books, including six about his adopted state of Colorado. A former department store executive, he is active in conservation issues, civic affairs, photography instruction and the publishing industry. Fielder and his family live in Greenwood Village.

Contents 4

Sponsors' Index 6

Introduction 11

Foreword 13

Dedication 15

REGIONAL BASKETBALL HISTORY

Hoop Heritage of the Wild, Wild West 16

Colorado's AAU Tournaments 21

Wyoming's 1943 NCAA Championship 30

Cinderella (Utah) Took the Train 34

Colorado's Final Four Years 38

Lady Buffs 42

THE MEDIA AND REGIONAL BASKETBALL

Regional Basketball on Radio & TV 46

Final Four and the National Media 49

CBS and the Final Four 52

Black and White and Technicolor Memories 54

ONE ROAD TO THE DENVER OLYMPIC TRYOUTS

Indiana/Kentucky Basketball 57

Oscar Robertson 60

Denver's 1960 Olympic Tryouts — The Best Ever 65

REGIONAL BASKETBALL TODAY

Colorado High School Basketball 70

The Mile High Classic 74

1985 and 1989 NCAA West Regional Tournament 80

The Denver Nuggets 86

Advertising Section 92

Volunteers 142-143

Acknowledgements 144

ISBN Number: 0-929969-12-X
Library of Congress Number: 89-051440

Published by Westcliffe Publishers, 2650 South Zuni Street, Englewood, Colorado 80110.

THE DENVER ORGANIZING COMMITTEE

WISHES TO EXPRESS ITS SINCERE GRATITUDE TO

THE PEPSI COLA BOTTLING COMPANY

FOR ITS SPONSORSHIP OF THIS BOOK,

ROCKY MOUNTAIN BASKETBALL

NAISMITH TO NINETEEN-NINETY

WELCOME COMMITTEE SPONSORS & CONTRIBUTORS INDEX

Ancient glaciers are responsible for the carving of alpine valleys in the Weminuche Wilderness Area, San Juan Mountains. Photo courtesy of John Fielder, from Colorado Lost Places and Forgotten Words.

The Denver Organizing Committee thanks the many sponsors and contributors whose generous support will make 1990 in Denver the ultimate Final Four. Advertisers' listings are followed by the page number in this book on which their advertisement appears.

Always Buy Colorado

AMI PRESBYTERIAN/ST. LUKE'S MEDICAL CENTER, page 92

ARA Leisure Services, Inc., page 93

Atech Piedmont Beef

BCS Financial Corporation

Best Stores

Blue Cross and Blue Shield of Colorado

Boettcher & Company

Boettcher Foundation

Boys Clubs of Metro Denver, Inc., page 95

Bradley Petroleum, Inc., page 96

Brock/Cook, Cook and Sons, page 97

Brooklyn's Restaurant

The Brown Palace Hotel

Campro Systems, Ltd., page 115

Capitol Engraving, page 98

Cattlemen's Group, Inc.

Central Bank of Denver, page 99

Cherry Hills Country Club

Colorado Economic Development Commission

Colorado Tourism Board

Colorado Wyoming Restaurant Association

Complete Printing & Envelope Company

CompreCare, page 100

Continental Airlines

Adolph Coors Company, page 101

Daniels & Associates, Inc., page 102

Nick Davidson, Inc.

Dean Witter

Deloitte Haskins + Sells, page 103

The Denver Athletic Club, page 104

City of Denver, page 105

Denver Marriott Southeast

Denver Merchandise Mart, page 107

Denver Metro Convention & Visitors Bureau

Denver Nuggets

Denver Organizing Committee, page 106

Denver Partnership

The Denver Post

Denver's TV 2 (KWGN), page 108

Dixon Paper, page 109

DowBrands, page 110

First Interstate of Ft. Collins

FLS Services, Inc., page 111

Foundation Mortgage/Jeff Heider, page 112

Frederic Printing Co.

Freeman Decorating

Gannett Outdoor of Colorado

Gart Brothers Sporting Goods, page 113

The Gates Corporation

The Greater Denver Chamber of Commerce

Hensel Phelps Construction Co., page 114

Holme Roberts & Owen, page 116

Hyatt Regency Beaver Creek

Marquis/Hyatt Regency Denver, page 121

Hyatt Regency Tech Center

IBM Corporation

Ideal Basic Industries, Inc.

Imperial Headwear

Information Handling Services, page 117

IDS Financial, page 120

The International

Janus Fund, page 119

The Stuart-James Company, Inc.

Joslins

Karsh & Hagan Advertising

K-BIG Sports Radio 1090, page 118

King Soopers

Kirkland & Ellis

KMGH TV

KOA Newsradio 85

Larrick Corporation

Marlowe's

Marriott Hotel City Center

Martin Marietta Astronautics, page 122

May D&F

MCI Telecommunications Corp., page 123

Miller Stockman Western Wear, page 124

Monfort of Colorado, Inc.

Moser Printing, page 125

MultiMedia Group, page 126

Nelowet Business Machines, Ltd.

Oldsmobile

One Tabor Center/Trammel Crowe, page 127

Outdoor Systems Advertising

Panorama Park, page 128

Pepsi Cola Bottling Company

Pontiac Division, General Motors Corporation

POULAN/WEED EATER

Prime Sports Network

Professional Travel Corporation, page 129

ProFusion Systems, Inc.

Public Service Company of Colorado, page 130

Radisson Hotel Denver, page 131

Robinson Dairy

Rocky Mountain News, page 132

Samsonite Corp., pages 94, 133

Sheraton Denver Airport Hotel, page 134

The Ski Train

Stouffer Concourse Hotel

Subaru

Gordon Swanson

Robert W. Taylor Design, Inc.

Titan Capital Corp., page 135

Touche Ross & Co., page 136

United Bank, page 137

US West Communications, page 138

Vail Associates

Village Inn, page 139

Warwick Hotel, page 140

WATERSAVER COMPANY, INC.

Westcliffe Publishers, Inc., page 141

Western Distributing Co.

Westin Hotel Tabor Center Denver

Windsor Financial Group, Ltd.

Winter Park Resort

The Writer Agency

YMCA of Metro Denver, page 97

11
Seton Hall
24
The Hall

Opposite: Seton Hall and Indiana University at the 1989 NCAA West Regional Tournament at Denver's McNichols Sports Arena. Photo courtesy of Rich Clarkson/ Sports Illustrated.

Sean Elliott, University of Arizona, was the 1989 NCAA Player of the Year. Arizona and the University of Nevada-Las Vegas were the other two teams at the 1989 NCAA West Regional Tournament in Denver. Photo courtesy of Rich Clarkson/ Sports Illustrated.

Rawlings
NCAA

I N T R O D U C T I O N

Basketball, Rocky Mountain style, has enjoyed a colorful run since James Naismith brought his new-fangled sport to Denver in 1895. Indeed, while he was the physical education director at the Mile High City's YMCA, Naismith began to refine "basket-ball" — the game he had invented in Springfield, Massachusetts, four years earlier.

When Naismith left Denver, bound for the University of Kansas, the seeds of his legacy were already taking root in the Rockies. Naismith's new game, designed as a simple physical diversion, had struck a chord in the hearts of many sports enthusiasts who had crossed his path in Colorado. Soon, the area was filled with basketball ambassadors.

While basketball in this region undoubtedly received a boost from Naismith's stint in Denver, many others also have left their imprint on Rocky Mountain basketball. This book, while just a glimpse, is a celebration of those people and places, which together, have put an indelible stamp on "hoops" in the Rockies.

****

It's a time to celebrate in 1990. It's also a year filled with memories of those who have contributed to our rich basketball heritage. For many, basketball is a passion, a true labor of love. Such was the case with the production of this book. The contributors, each uniquely qualified to present their subjects, have generously donated their work.

Here's hoping you enjoy it!

— Roger Kinney, General Chairman
The Denver Organizing Committee

***Roger Kinney** is the general chairman of the Denver Organizing Committee. He has served in that capacity since 1983, when Denver's bid for the 1990 Final Four was submitted to the NCAA.*

He was born and reared in Denver, played basketball and baseball for Denver East High, and baseball for the University of Colorado. He is a graduate of the University of Colorado and holds an MBA from the University of Denver.

He has long been active in metropolitan sports activities, serving as the chairman of the Metro Sports Committee of the Denver Chamber of Commerce, president of the Greater Denver Junior Golf Association, and treasurer of the Colorado Sports Hall of Fame. Kinney has also served as a coach and administrator for the Old Timers Baseball Association, the Young American League, the Southeast Little League and the YMCA Youth Basketball program.

Roger and his wife, Sue, and their three children live in Englewood.

TOURNAMENT SOUVENI
ARE ON SALE NOW
Rocky Mountain News
Every Morning
WALKER
34
NCAA

F O R E W O R D

Opposite: Finals of the 1985 West Regionals at McNichols Sports Arena. Kentucky was the ultimate victor. Photo courtesy of Rich Clarkson/Sports Illustrated.

Colorado State University's 1987-88 team finished second in the National Invitational Tournament (NIT) in New York City. Photo courtesy of CSU's Sports Information Department.

Basketball in the Rocky Mountain region carries a proud heritage. Long before there were any Broncos, Bears or Zephyrs, Dr. Naismith's game reached such a level of popularity that Denver proclaimed itself the "basketball capital of the world."

That boast was not without justification. It highlighted the fact that before there was an event such as the Final Four tournament with all its hysteria, the week-long National AAU Tournament was playing to standing-room-only crowds and attracting teams from coast to coast. This remarkable "derby of dribble" was an annual event for Denver, and it produced many of the players who would become the foundation of US Olympic basketball teams for the better part of two decades.

It also isn't surprising that basketball has been the ticket for a great many inductees into the Colorado Sports Hall of Fame. We aren't talking about your ordinary, garden variety celebrities. We're talking about authentic sports heroes who have left indelible marks on the sports history of the Rocky Mountain region. Most notable are the legendary Ace Gruenig and Jack McCracken, who were synonymous with Denver basketball from 1933 through 1949. Gruenig was named to ten AAU All-America teams and McCracken to eight before they were both elected to the Hall of Fame in 1968.

Other basketball luminaries in the hall include Vince Boryla and Burdie Haldorson, who were All-Americans and Olympians; the University of Denver's All-American Byron Beck, who was a mainstay of the old Denver Rockets; the Denver Nuggets' Dan Issel; and record-setting coaches Harry Simmons, Jim Darden, Jim Baggott and Roy Byers.

The National AAU Tournament holds a special significance for me because I participated as a player, coach, referee and administrator for some 20 years. In fact, I had the unique distinction of being the only person ever to participate as both a player and coach for different teams in the same tournament when my 1948 Regis College team qualified for the event while I played for the AAU Denver team. Fortunately, we were placed in opposite brackets, so I never had to face the dilemma of coaching against myself.

Much of the attention in the early days was focused on the National AAU Tournament, since it was the only game in town. But the region's college teams had their moments of glory too. Burdie Haldorson led the University of Colorado Buffaloes into the Final Four in Kansas City, only to lose to Bill Russell's San Francisco Dons. Colorado State turned out some championship teams during the Bill Green and Boyd Grant years. Vince Boryla brought prosperity to the University of Denver. The Air Force Academy Falcons were exciting when high-scoring Bob Beckel, who's now a general, led the attack. And up in Laramie, Ev Shelton's Wyoming Cowboys were a perennial national power.

But the big story of the late 1940s was written by a small band of Regis College Rangers who capped a 36-3 season in 1949 by winning the National Catholic Tournament in Denver and finishing second in the NAIA Tournament in Kansas City. Dubbed the "Buzz Boys" thanks to their swarming defense and fast-breaking offense, the Rangers piled up 105 wins against just 33 losses from 1946 through 1960.

Today, the Final Four tournament is the crowning touch to the rich basketball heritage in the Rocky Mountains. The Colorado Sports Hall of Fame heartily welcomes the tournament to Denver and salutes the Organizing Committee including chairman Roger Kinney and his capable and dedicated volunteers. We hope this historic moment will be the springboard for many more years of Hall of Fame-style basketball in the Rocky Mountain region!

— Larry Varnell, President
Colorado Sports Hall of Fame

D E D I C A T I O N

"I often tell my players that next to my own flesh and blood, they are the closest to me. They are my children. I get wrapped up in them, their lives, and their problems."

— John Wooden, *They Call Me Coach*

Perhaps no group has made a more positive impact on Rocky Mountain basketball than the dedicated men and women who coach the game.

Many times, the best of what's good in this life emanates from the most basic of relationships, such as parent and child, husband and wife. That's also the case in the world of basketball where a natural link exists between player and coach.

Floyd Theard

Coaches have the unique opportunity to fill many roles for players in their formative years, including teacher, counselor, parental figure and confidant. The best coaches care deeply, not only about basketball, but also about the young men and women they coach. To these coaches, the highest compliment they can receive is that they improved the lives of those who played for them. For Bill Weimar and Floyd Theard, that description is a fitting epitaph.

Weimar was a native Coloradoan who played high school ball in Colorado Springs and college ball at the University of Denver. He then coached for 28 years in the Denver Prep League, compiling a 315-165 record, before finishing his career at DU's helm. More importantly, he gained respect in the basketball community for his kindness, integrity and compassion for young people.

Weimar also was a champion of basketball in our region, being the first to offer his support and guidance when Denver began the application process for the NCAA Final Four. He passed away in October of 1987.

Theard also coached in the Denver Prep League and at DU where he fashioned a 107-38 record over five years. Indeed, he never had a losing season, putting together a career mark of 143-60. Despite that glowing win-loss record, his true legacy is the class with which he conducted himself while displaying the qualities of leadership and sportsmanship. He was another good friend of Rocky Mountain basketball and an enthusiastic volunteer and team host for the 1985 Regionals in Denver. He died in April of 1985.

We miss Bill Weimar and Floyd Theard for their coaching ability, friendly counsel, and enthusiastic support of the game. Basketball in the Rockies today is much the better as a result of the years they spent practicing their craft.

Bill Weimar

Opposite: Barn and hoop, White River National Forest, Colorado. Photo courtesy of John Fielder.

HOOP HERITAGE OF THE WILD, WILD WEST

KEVIN SIMPSON

James Naismith invented basketball, using peach baskets, a soccer ball and nine-man teams, as a classroom assignment to devise a game that could be played indoors between football and baseball seasons. Photo courtesy of the Metro Denver YMCA.

In the evolution of sport, circumstances conspire in mysterious ways.

A rotating ball defies the laws of physics and gives birth to the curveball. A badly outmuscled football team improvises the fórward pass. And in Denver, three circumstances converge at the optimum moment to lend character and soul to a game in its infancy.

James Naismith, basketball and the rough-and-tumble West, like three friends in search of their future, forge a lasting relationship in a land fertile for progress.

To be sure, James Naismith *was* the game of basketball as it existed in those rough-hewn, formative stages long before the advent of the hoop accouterments we now take for granted: collapsible rims, alley-oops, Dick Vitale. And so, if Springfield, Massachusetts can claim its rightful place in history as the cradle of basketball, the Rocky Mountain West at least provided the game's playpen once Naismith migrated to Denver in 1895 to work at the local YMCA.

It was in the rollicking West of the 1890s, where gold and silver dreams were born on mining claims along the Continental Divide, that Naismith fine-tuned the game he had invented only a few years before at Springfield College.

In some ways, Naismith probably would look at today's game, with all its ceremonial trappings and partisanship, and shudder in amazement. This wasn't at all what he'd had in mind when he nailed up the peach baskets and sent two nine-man teams into battle with a soccer ball. In fact, he hinted at his recreational ideal when he addressed a YMCA convention in Cañon City in 1896.

"Some people say we should have no competitive athletics," he said. "Competitive work is used simply for the glorification of the person, the club or the college. If a man is almost breaking a record, the world is looking at him, and he will try to do his best. Boys used to box because people would look at them and applaud. When they were compelled to go into a room by themselves they soon gave it up. . . . Remember the distinction between association athletics and the athletic clubs."

A record of the YMCA proceedings noted that Naismith's speech was followed by "an interesting game of basketball." A team representing the Pueblo YMCA lost a squeaker to a team from Colorado College, 6-2. Obviously crude by today's athletic standards, the exhibition, nonetheless, underscored the thrust of Naismith's passion for competitive athletics: The sport is the thing. In later years, he upheld that conviction as he watched in dismay as his game entered the professional arena.

"It's an amateur's game, invented by an amateur, and everyone should have a chance to play it," Naismith once said.

It was a noble creed set forth by a man whose motivation for success — indeed, his decision to head west to Denver in the first

In contrast to this dignified portrait, early newspaper articles described basketball as "an uproarious game that was accompanied by much yelling and undignified cheering." Photo courtesy of Springfield College.

Basketball prospered in the Rocky Mountain Region as seen here in a championship game at the Violet Street Playground (city unknown), circa 1910. Photo courtesy of the Colorado Historical Society.

place — grew from a desire to mold himself into something of an athletic Renaissance man.

The Canadian-born Naismith determined early in his life that he would root his worldly pursuits in religion. When he moved to the YMCA Training School in Springfield, he sought to foster both physical and spiritual strength in his students. Eventually, his interests expanded with his exposure to the inevitable injuries that resulted from competition. Naismith decided to go back to school and become a doctor.

The fact that he and his wife, Maude, already had a young daughter meant he would have to spread himself thin between career and family life. But Naismith forged ahead with his medical school plans and sought a situation that would allow him to attend school and still feed three hungry mouths — preferably with work at a YMCA gymnasium.

Naismith's basketball legacy lived on after he left Denver. Photo courtesy of the Colorado Historical Society, Agnes F. Miner Collection.

In the summer of 1895, the pieces fell together perfectly. Naismith was offered the job of director of physical education at the Denver YMCA and was accepted into the Gross Medical School, which later consolidated with the University of Denver and University of Colorado medical schools.

Although the central branch of the Denver YMCA already was the largest in the country, Naismith became its first physical director when the association moved into new quarters in the Florence Building at 18th and Champa streets. Officials noted at the time of his hiring that Naismith was "a man of wide experience and rare ability . . . and is the originator of the popular game of basketball."

As a 34-year-old freshman medical student, he set about juggling his studies with his duties at the YMCA. Occasionally, he refereed local basketball tournaments and, from that helpful vantage point, revised the rules that originally had been typed on a single sheet of paper as part of a school assignment to invent an indoor game to play between football and baseball seasons. Perhaps most significantly, the unwieldy nine-member teams gradually were reduced to seven and finally five, despite the contention from some quarters that devoting an entire gym to 10 athletes constituted an unforgivable waste of resources.

While Naismith balanced his studies and his job and tinkered with basketball, his wife gave birth to their second child on December 21, 1897. The date is significant only because historians note that Helen Naismith arrived on the sixth anniversary of basketball's birth. And like the game, she proved a loud and raucous infant.

"Helen Naismith? More like Hell 'n' Blazes," her father said.

Similarly, basketball spread like wildfire throughout the West, inciting fiery passions as it grew in popularity. One early player at the YMCA recalled that the duties of the team captain included making sure that a locker room window remained unlocked in case players and referees needed to beat a hasty retreat from irate fans.

Such was the character of Naismith's game. Modern self-proclaimed purists who cringe at today's violent slam-dancing beneath the basket should note that Naismith never intended basketball to be a genteel pursuit whistled to a temporary standstill by aggressive physical contact.

The originator's early rule revisions kept intact many similarities the game bore to rugby — particularly its rugged temperament. Some YMCA officials fretted over what early newspaper clippings described as "an uproarious game that was accompanied by much yelling and undignified cheering." Now, on its best days, basketball achieves the exact qualities that worried its early detractors.

The beginning of the end of Naismith's three-year stay in Denver came as he gave athletic instruction at the YMCA, but it had nothing to do with his fledgling sport. Naismith was teaching a tumbling class when a student miscalculated an aerial somersault and died of a broken neck. For months, Naismith lived on the edge of despair. He described a tortured sleep repeatedly interrupted by nightmares that replayed the tragedy in his mind's eye.

He would be jolted from sleep, dripping with sweat and, as he recalled, "shaking like a tree in a windstorm." When the visions appeared more frequently, he feared he was going insane. Naismith finally knelt in the gymnasium at the exact spot of the tragedy and prayed for guidance.

A few days later, he got a phone call from Amos Alonzo Stagg, who had coached Naismith in football at the Springfield YMCA before moving on to the University of Chicago. Stagg had suggested Naismith for the position of chapel director at the University of Kansas in Lawrence. Stagg's telegram to the KU president read: "Recommend James Naismith, inventor of basketball, medical doctor, Presbyterian minister, teetotaler, all-around athlete, non-smoker, and owner of vocabulary without cuss words. Address YMCA, Denver, Colorado."

Naismith accepted the development as the answer to his prayer. He never returned to Colorado to live, but on trips back to the state, he faithfully visited the site of the tumbler's death in the YMCA gym. Always, he would kneel and pray.

Naismith always emphasized the importance of the sport over the individual. Photo courtesy of the Metro Denver YMCA.

Although Naismith left Denver, his basketball legacy lived on. The game prospered in the region and particularly at the YMCA, which, in 1900, fielded a team called the Victors coached by local insurance man S.G. Tracy. The six players who comprised that club journeyed to the 1904 World's Fair in St. Louis to play a team from Chicago that billed itself as the national champion. The Victors prevailed.

Meanwhile, Naismith arrived in Lawrence to find the athletic department in such a sorry state that he considered returning to Denver. But he overcame his frustration, and despite the fact that he'd been hired more for his religious background than for his status as basketball's inventor, his introduction of the game to KU laid the groundwork for the University's burgeoning interest in sports.

Naismith didn't remain a stranger to Colorado, though. His oldest daughter, Margaret, settled with her husband in Ordway and frequently received her parents as visitors. When the Amateur Athletic Union national tournament moved from Kansas City to Denver in 1935, Naismith was invited as guest of honor to watch the field eliminated to the two teams that would represent the AAU in the Olympic tryouts. He had hoped for a strong performance from the Denver Safeways — partly because Denver had been his home for three years and partly because the players were reputed to be YMCA members, and therefore, products of his legacy at the Y. To his disappointment, the Safeways didn't even reach the finals.

Even so, Naismith's return was a triumphant one. He was paraded before 4,000 fans, introduced along with the men he had coached during his tenure at the Denver YMCA, and presented with a gold medal for his life's work. He told the crowd, "I only wish I could say with my lips what is in my heart."

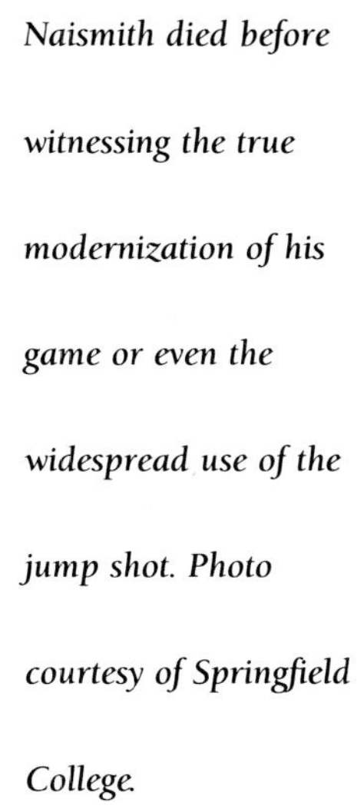

Naismith died before witnessing the true modernization of his game or even the widespread use of the jump shot. Photo courtesy of Springfield College.

Two years later, he did speak his mind. In the winter of 1938, while visiting his daughter in Ordway, Naismith ventured back to Denver to watch the Safeways in action. The evolution of his game must have disappointed him because in that very month, he caused a stir by denouncing recent revisions in the rules — particularly one that demanded the offensive team cross the halfcourt line within 10 seconds. The only revisions he favored were changes designed to eliminate or offset the advantage held by taller players.

But the game's course had been charted and the revisions would continue for years. Some, like the three-point field goal, significantly offset the advantage of size, as Naismith had hoped. However, his death in 1939 at age 78 kept him from witnessing the true modernization of the game or even the widespread use of the jump shot.

Essentially, though, his invention remained intact. Each spring, when tournament fever grips a nation, gymnasiums across the country erupt in celebration of a game that still displays signs of its Wild West heritage — an uproarious game accompanied by much yelling and undignified cheering.

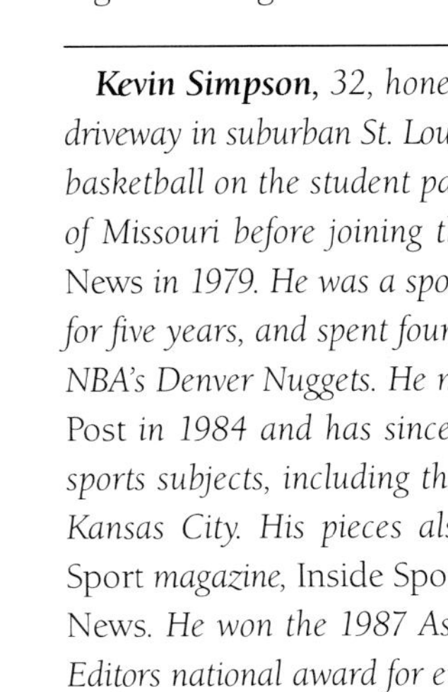

Kevin Simpson, *32, honed his jump shot on a driveway in suburban St. Louis and covered college basketball on the student paper at the University of Missouri before joining the* Rocky Mountain News *in 1979. He was a sportswriter at the* News *for five years, and spent four of them covering the NBA's Denver Nuggets. He moved to* The Denver Post *in 1984 and has since covered a variety of sports subjects, including the 1987 Final Four in Kansas City. His pieces also have appeared in* Sport *magazine,* Inside Sports *and* The Sporting News. *He won the 1987 Associated Press Sports Editors national award for enterprise reporting for a series of stories on the plight of Native American athletes.*

DENVER - 50 MILLION B.C.
HOW THE GAME WAS REALLY INVENTED

SEE... I TOLD YA IT'D BEAT THE HECK OUTTA THAT STUPID WHEEL IDEA OF YOURS.

Drew Litton
ROCKY MOUNTAIN NEWS

***Drew Litton**, of the* Rocky Mountain News *is one of the nation's only full-time sports editorial cartoonists. Five days a week, he specializes in hard-edged commentary on controversial sports issues.*

Litton, now 30, was reared in El Paso, Texas, and attended the University of Texas at El Paso, where he created the award-winning comic strip "The Classes Quo." After graduation, he worked at the El Paso Times *as a staff artist before joining the* Rocky Mountain News *in 1982.*

Litton is syndicated twice a week by United Features and NEA. He was a nominee for the 1989 Reuben Award and recently won the Colorado Sigma Delta Chi award in the editorial cartoon category.

A collection of his cartoons titled "win, lose & Drew" was published in February of 1987 by the Denver Publishing Company.

Litton and his wife, Debbie, live in Littleton.

COLORADO'S AAU TOURNAMENTS

BUD MALONEY

AAU Logo from All-American Dick Wells' 1938 uniform.

In the dark Depression days of the mid-1930s, when national unemployment was as high as 20 percent, the only prominent professional sports in America were major and minor league baseball and the fledgling National Football League.

Professional basketball had made a few attempts to gain a foothold along the eastern seaboard, but the game's first real success, the National Basketball Association, was not to blossom until after World War II.

Collegiate football was the king of the sports pages in the fall and collegiate basketball got its share of newspaper space in the winter before pro baseball took over in the spring and summer. Track and field, pretty much as today, surfaced every four years at the Olympics.

Yet, there always had been a yearning among athletes for post-graduate competition. There had long been YMCA basketball teams and sandlot baseball and football teams. When the Depression hit, there still was that yearning for competition. Team sponsors, if not jobs, were available and the better athletes went from Frank Merriwell amateurism to picking up a few dollars for their talents.

Semipro baseball teams, usually merchant-sponsored, were in every village and town. Everybody made a few bucks and hard-throwing pitchers with good curveballs could live quite handsomely. Fast-pitch softball, a sport that boomed during the Depression, had ready money and, sometimes, jobs for windmill pitchers who could whiz the ball past hitters.

Barnstorming basketball teams were everywhere. The Harlem Globetrotters got their start in the 1930s and the bearded House of David had one team playing in the West and another in the East. Amateur basketball flourished in the same way under the sponsorship of the National Amateur Athletic Union, particularly in that vast and nebulous area of the Midwest known as the Missouri Valley.

The National AAU basketball tournament, with its origins in New York, had been played since before the turn of the century, but by the mid-1920s, the tourney had become firmly established in Kansas City. From 1921 through 1934, all but one of the AAU champions came from Missouri, Oklahoma and Kansas. In the 1930s, however, the Kansas City tournament, like all other sports of the time, was having trouble selling tickets and in 1935, Denver was introduced to this basketball extravaganza for the first time.

From 1935 — when W.N. "Bill" Haraway brought the finest of all amateur basketball players, Bob "Ace" Gruenig, to Denver — until the late 1960s, the Mile High City was the amateur basketball capital of the universe. Willard N. "Big Bill" Greim was the tournament director, a position he held throughout the tourney's stay in Colorado which lasted until 1968, when it was moved to Macon, Georgia.

The 6'8" Gruenig, who had never played college ball, was with the Lifschultz Fast Freight team out of Chicago during the last Kansas

City tournament in 1934, which Haraway witnessed with the Denver entry. Although the Fast Freighters had a fast derailment, Haraway convinced Gruenig that his playing future was in Colorado. And so he became the center for Denver's Safeway-Piggly Wiggly Grocery Stores' team, coached by Glen Jacobs, when the 1935 tournament began on a court painted on the City Auditorium stage.

With Gruenig and Jack McCracken, a 6'2 1/2" guard from Maryville State Teachers College in Missouri, the Safeway-Piggly Wiggly team was an immediate success, and so was the tournament. For a week in late March, Denver was a mecca of dribbling and shooting as up to 60 teams came to play, representing AAU districts from New York to San Diego and Seattle to Miami.

Denver's 1934 Piggly Wiggly-Safeway team featuring W.N. "Bill" Haraway (in business suit) and team captain Jack McCracken (inset). In 1935 the AAU tournament moved to Denver. Photo courtesy of Frank Haraway.

Play would begin on Sunday morning on the Auditorium stage, its baskets attached to the balconies on each side. Games were scheduled all day and continued on Monday and Tuesday to set the stage, so to speak, for Wednesday's round of eight games that stretched from early morning to midnight.

The quarterfinals — the best bargain of the week when the finest eight amateur teams in the country squared off — were scheduled for Thursday evening, while the semifinals were on Friday. The championship game was played on Saturday.

Some 6,578 fans jammed the Auditorium on that first Thursday night of play in 1935, and the average attendance for seven days was 4,700. The gross gate was $20,602, which netted the AAU $6,615. That doesn't sound like much now, but this was at the height of the Depression when the country was so poor that the big entertainment attractions were "bank night" at the movies (admission 25 cents) or Monopoly at home with the neighbors.

The take might have been greater in that first tournament, but Gruenig and McCracken bowed out in the quarterfinals when Safeway-Piggly Wiggly lost to the Kansas City Stage Lines, 30-28. Four of the eight seeded teams were from Kansas, Missouri and Oklahoma, and they all gained the quarterfinals. Three of them reached the semifinals before the Stage Lines downed the Globe Refiners of McPherson, Kansas, 45-26, in the championship contest.

Interestingly, games in that 1935 tournament were played under the center-jump rule, as were 1936 and 1937 contests. The rule, abandoned in 1938, had the players return to center court for a jump ball after every basket.

One of the stars of the 1935 Stage Lines team was Omar "Bud" Browning, who later played with and coached the Phillips 66 teams into the 1960s. That first Denver tournament All-America team included Browning and Herman Fischer of the Stage Lines, College Joe Fortenberry and Francis Johnson of the Refiners, and Chuck Hyatt of Hollywood's Universal Pictures team. Hyatt later would coach Phillips 66 with Browning and count among his horses the 6'8" Fortenberry, who would go on to have legendary under-the-basket battles with Gruenig.

Gruenig and McCracken eventually would bring three national championships to Denver, the first one under coach Ev Shelton in 1937, and Gruenig would play 14 seasons, through 1948, making the AAU All-America team 10 times. McCracken was named All-America five times and remained active through the 1948 season. No player ever approached Gruenig's record and only two Phillips stars, seven-foot tall Bob "Foothills" Kurland and Gordon "Shorty" Carpenter, exceeded McCracken's five All-America listings, winning honors six times.

Only five other players made All-America as many as four times. They include Burdie Haldorson, who first made it with the Cinderella Luckett-Nix team of 1955, and then with Phillips; Jimmy "Scat" McNatt of Phillips; Don Barksdale, who played for several Oakland teams; Frank McCabe of the Peoria Caterpillars and Bill Reigel, who made it twice each with the McDonald Scots of Lake Charles, Louisiana, and the Akron Goodyears.

The Denver tournament was played on the Auditorium stage through 1952 (glass backboards were introduced in 1948) and the action was moved to the adjacent Auditorium Arena for the 1953 tournament. It landed at the larger Denver Coliseum in 1960. When attendance began to lag, the tourney was moved back to the Auditorium Arena in 1964, where it stayed until the end.

The Missouri Valley never lost its tournament influence, largely through the efforts of Phillips 66. Teams from the heartland entered each year and many credit Vickers Oil from Wichita with helping to revive the game in the late 1950s by having two seven footers, Wade "Swede" Halbrook, 7'4", and Don Boldebuck, at 7'2", play together for the first time at any level.

Denver, of course, was the hub, but the city never had the kind of sponsorship that Phillips 66, the Peoria Cats and the Goodyear Wingfoots out of Akron had. The Mile High City's national championships came when Safeway Stores sponsored the 1937 team, the civic Denver Nuggets took the 1939 title, and the American Legion squad ran away with the 1942 flag.

The 1957-58 Phillips 66 team. Photo Courtesy of The Denver Public Library, Western History Collection.

After that first Safeway-Piggly Wiggly squad of 1935 played itself out, Safeway sponsored a team through 1938. The Nuggets picked it up for two years, and then the Legion for three years. In 1944, the Ambrose Jellymakers combined with the Legion and then took over as sole sponsor in 1945 and 1946. The Nuggets returned for two years before the Denver Chevrolet dealers — largely through the influence of Russ Lyons, who was the National AAU basketball chairman — provided sponsorship from 1949 to 1951. Then came Central Bank & Trust, with Max Brooks the driving force, from 1952 through 1956. Many of the players established themselves as businessmen with the Chevrolet dealers and Central Bank and remained with those companies through their working lives.

The Denver-Chicago Trucking Co., under the operation of George Kolowich, took the team

in 1957 and stayed through 1963. The last five Denver entries were hastily thrown together aggregations backed by Capitol Federal Savings. Denver's best teams played under those banners, but in the days of the 50-team tournaments, as many as six regional quintets would be among the entries, including squads from the Denver Athletic Club, Kansas City Life Insurance, Continental Airlines, Eaton Metal, Coors, Murphy-Mahoney Chevrolet, Jussel Electric and the University of Denver. Teams also came from around the state, such as Fort Collins Nash, Martin Jewelers of Colorado Springs, White Palace of Fort Collins and Gregory Clothing of Greeley, as well as those two unforgettable Cinderella teams, Poudre Valley Creamery of Fort Collins and Luckett-Nix Barbershop of Boulder.

Beginning with that first national title in 1937, Denver's primary team — be it Safeway, the Nuggets, the Legion or whoever — played in the championship game eight times in nine years. Phillips 66 first played in the tournament in 1937, and it was largely because of the 66ers that the Denver representatives usually fell one step short of winning.

Indeed, in that stretch from 1937 to 1945, Denver and Phillips played for the AAU Championship eight times. All three of Denver's titles were won over Phillips teams, and when the 66ers finished first in 1940, 1943, 1944 and 1945, Denver was the victim. In 1938, Denver's Safeway team lost in the championship game to the Kansas City Healeys after Phillips lost to the Healeys in the semifinals.

The "Year of the West Coast" came in 1941 when 20th Century Fox from Hollywood with Frank Lubin — one of the brightest AAU stars — defeated the Olympic Club of San Francisco, whose lineup featured the fabled Hank Luisetti, fresh out of Stanford University. Lubin, a monster of a man at 6'7", was always the heavy when he played in Denver, but in his later days, it became a question of whether the railbirds really disliked him or just loved to razz ol' Frankenstein.

The AAU National Championship was first won by the Denver Safeways in 1937, left to right: Foot Masteller, Werner Frank, Jack McCracken, business manager George Scruggs, Lew Young, Safeway division manager Tom Henritze, Ace Gruenig, coach Ev Shelton, Tex Colvin, Duck Dowell, Jimmy Bauer, Joe Fee. Photo courtesy of Frank Haraway.

Except for 1941 Gruenig made the All-America team each year in that nine-year stretch and McCracken was named five times. Other Denver All-America players included Tex Colvin, Dick Wells, Tee Connelley, Bill Strannigan, Bob Doll, Bob Marsh, George Hamburg, Bob Marks and Jack Harvey. Phillips' All-Americans included Fortenberry, McNatt, Carpenter, Luisetti, Grady Lewis, Don Lockard, Bill Martin, Paul Lindemann, Jay Wallenstrom, Ray Ebling and Fred Pralle.

After 1942, Denver never won another title, being turned away in the championship game nine times. In addition to the losses to Phillips in 1943, 1944 and 1945, final game defeats came in 1948, 1958, 1961, 1962, 1963 and 1965. There also were six losses in the semifinals, and another six eliminations in the quaterfinals.

In beating Denver in 1943, 1944 and 1945, Phillips began a run of six consecutive championships, the longest in AAU history, with Kurland, Marty Nash, R.C. Pitts and Cab Renick running the Phillips' steamroller. In all, the 66ers were to win 11 titles, by far the most of any team playing in Denver's 33 tournaments.

When the Safeways won Denver's first championship in 1937, Gruenig, McCracken, Colvin, Werner Frank and Duck Dowell were the starters, while Jimmy Bauer was the only significant sub. The score in the championship game was tied, 37-37, with 7 1/2 minutes to play when McCracken's free throw put Denver ahead to stay. Colvin and Dowell then tipped in missed shots to make it 42-37, and the Safeways stalled it out to win, 43-38. Dowell led the Denver scoring with 11 points, Gruenig had 10 and McCracken and Colvin collected nine points each. Gruenig, McCracken and Colvin made the All-America team.

In 1939, the Nuggets, again playing with six men — Gruenig, McCracken, Connelley, Wells, Colvin and Ralph Bishop — played great defense to take out the 66ers, 25-22. Connelley held Pralle, the most valuable player of the 1938 tourney, scoreless, and Gruenig limited

The Denver-Chicago Trucking Company took over sponsorship of the Denver team from 1957-1963. The team had disappointing second-round losses in 1957 and 1960, but reached the championship game in 1958, 1961 and 1962. Photo courtesy of the Denver Public Library, Western History Collection.

Fortenberry to one hoop. Connelley's shot from the corner opened the scoring and the Nuggets led all the way. But it wasn't until Gruenig made two free throws in the closing seconds that Denver clinched the game. Gruenig led the Nuggets' scoring with nine points, while Ray Ebling had 11 for Phillips.

In 1942, the Legion again used only six players — Gruenig, McCracken, Strannigan, Marsh, Harvey and Marks — in pulling away from Phillips in the second half to win, 45-32. Gruenig had eight baskets and four free throws for 20 points, and Marsh, a first-rate defensive specialist, held Luisetti to four points. Again, Gruenig and McCracken as well as Strannigan — who chipped in with four baskets in the title game — were named All-Americans.

In 1945, Denver's Ambrose Jellymakers led the 66ers by 13 points, 40-27, with nine minutes to play, but Browning led a rally that powered Phillips to a last-minute win, 47-46. Frank Schwartzer, an unheralded Phillips reserve, scored the winning basket when he drove for a layup after a pass from McNatt.

Vince Boryla, Jimmy Darden and Roy Lipscomb were the standouts on excellent Nuggets teams in 1947 and 1948, but only twice in the next eight years did either the Chevs or Central Bank make it as far as the semifinals. Denver-Chicago had disappointing second-round losses in 1957 and 1960, but reached the championship game in 1958, 1961 and 1962 as Harv Schmidt, Barry Brown, Jimmy Ashmore, George Bon Salle, Terry Rand, Art Bunte, Mike Moran, Horace Walker, Joe Belmont, George Lee, Les Lane and Dennis Boone starred.

The Peoria Cats, who became the dominant team in the 1950s, won championships in 1952, 1953, 1954, 1958 and 1960, the last year of their existence. The Caterpillars produced All-America players in Dan Pippen, Ron Bontemps, Frank McCabe, Howie Williams, Dick Retherford, Bert Born, Howie Crittenden, Jim Palmer, Bob Boozer and Don Ohl, and because of their emergence, ranked second only to the 66ers on Denver fans' hate list.

The Cats' 1958 title came at the expense of Denver-Chicago in four overtimes, the longest game in tournament history. Chuck Wolfe, a left-hander from the University of North Dakota, wasn't among the Peoria all-timers, but he played his finest game in leading the Cats to a 74-71 triumph.

Over the years, the Pacific Coast produced talented amateur teams, with 20th Century Fox, the Oakland Bittners, the San Francisco Stewart Chevrolets and the Seattle Buchan Bakers all winning titles.

The service teams, quite naturally, began to appear in great numbers during World War II, and two of them — Colorado Springs Army and Ft. Warren, Wyoming — made it to the semifinals in 1944. The Ft. Lewis, Washington Warriors were in the quarterfinals in 1945 — the year that the Warriors' Gale Bishop set the all-time single-game scoring record of 62 points — and the Miramar, California Marines gained the quarterfinals in 1946.

By and large, however, the service clubs didn't have the size to go all the way, and except for 1957, it wasn't until the caliber of tournament play began to wane in the mid-1960s that the well-conditioned servicemen, deep in manpower, began to dominate. In 1957, a running bunch of Air Force All-Stars featuring Dick Boushka and Ron Tomsic, two veterans of AAU competition, defeated San Francisco's Olympic Club in the title game.

For sheer drama, perhaps the greatest night in tournament history came in the 1951 semifinals. In the first of the two games, Johnny O'Boyle, an obscure guard from Colorado State University who was playing for the Poudre Valley Creamery team, threw the ball three-quarters of the court for a basket to beat Peoria as the final gun went off. In the second game, the San Francisco Stewart Chevs — powered by George Yardley, Cliff Crandall and Frankie Kuzara, who would later play for Denver's Central Bank team — defeated Phillips in three overtimes, 66-63, in what was the longest game until the Peoria-Denver contest of 1958.

There have been quite a few upsets in tournament history, but perhaps none was more implausible than when a collection of Northwest collegians wearing the uniforms of Everybody's Drug from Eugene, Oregon became Everybody's Team by stopping the 66ers on a Wednesday afternoon in 1953, 66-52. Phillips was seeded second behind the defending champion Peoria Cats, but to the delight of 1,000 or so fans, the squad from Bartlesville was never in the game.

Only two of the Drugmen, Chet Noe and Jim Sugrue, went on to play with major amateur teams, and neither became a star. Still, Everybody's Drug had everybody in the Auditorium rooting for them in the quarterfinals, and they responded by beating Ritz Cafe of Carbondale, Illinois, 81-64. The enthusiasm continued in the semifinals, but Eugene had come as far as it could, finally losing to the Los Alamitos, California Naval Air Station, a team led by Yardley and Johnny Arndt.

Another memorable upset came in 1951 when a Dallas upstart, Vandegriff Motors, bumped the Oakland Blue 'n Gold, who had made it to the finals the previous two years. In

1956, Pasadena Mirror-Glaze, mostly stocked with players from Pasadena Nazarene College, eliminated Peoria in the first game of the Wednesday evening program.

In 1957, the McDonald Scots shocked the Mile High City by besting Denver-Chicago during the Wednesday evening program, and in 1958, Oklahoma's Ft. Leonard Wood, with a five-man team and virtually no height, beat the Wichita Vickers in the quarterfinals. The Scots, although little known at the time, had several major AAU-caliber players including the redoubtable Reigel. Ft. Leonard Wood was quarterbacked by K.C. Jones, who went on to greater fame as a Boston Celtics player and coach.

The most incredible upstarts were O'Boyle's Poudre Valley Creamery team in 1951 and Luckett-Nix in 1955, both reaching the finals with very talented young players. Glen Anderson and Bill Gossett, who were CSU standouts, were with Poudre Valley; later they moved to Central Bank. Luckett-Nix had Burdie Haldorson and Bob Jeangerard, who had just completed their eligibility at the University of Colorado. Both later played with the 66ers after making the 1956 Olympic team with Bill Russell. Jeangerard was with the Air Force All-Stars when they won the tournament in 1957, and Haldorson developed into the best shooting center since Gruenig.

When all roads for hundreds of basketball teams led to Denver and the National AAU Tournament, this Atlas Pacific Engineers team from Oakland was included. Photo courtesy of the Denver Public Library, Western History Collection.

Scoring came a long way in the tournament's Denver history. In the first Colorado-based tourney, the Globe Refiners rolled up the highest total — 53 — in a victory over the University of Denver. Two of the quarter-final winners that year scored only in the 30s, and no championship-game winner put up as many as 50 points until Phillips beat the Legion, 57-40, in 1943.

Gradually, scores climbed, and, as might be expected, Phillips was the first team to score 100 when it slaughtered a hapless Roanoke, Virginia quintet in 1947, 103-28.

Scores really began to explode in 1959 when 30-second clocks were used. Wichita's champions averaged 107 points a game and set a scoring record in the quarterfinals by beating the Baton Rouge, Louisiana Teamsters, 102-82.

A year later, Denver-Chicago broke the single-game record by thumping Cherry's Choke Boys from Little Rock, 122-63, in the first round. Vickers, however, established the all-time high with a 126-80 win over the Cheyenne Merchants in the second round. Vickers, favored to repeat its 1959 triumph, lost its next game in the quarterfinals to Seattle's Buchan Bakers, 93-83.

The only team to score more than 100 points and lose was the Army All-Star team of 1959, which Wichita bested in overtime in the semifinals, 104-102.

The greatest single-game individual performance in Denver tournament history came in 1945 when Gale Bishop, a former Washington State College star playing with the Ft. Lewis Warriors, poured in the then-amazing total of 62 points as his team walloped a bunch from Hoxie, Kansas, 87-21. Bishop, a 6'3" forward, sank 28 of 40 shots and made six of seven free throws. The former Cougar was an unusually fine leaper for his time, and on that historic evening, about half of his baskets came on tip-ins. Ironically, Bishop had broken his own record of 50 points, which he had set in the 1943 tourney.

Larry Toburen of DU holds third place in the scoring annals having clicked for 48 points against Boise Junior College in 1940. Gruenig has the fourth-highest total, established in the twilight of his career. The Acer had 42 points against the US Naval Academy while playing for the Murphy-Mahoney Graybeards in 1948. The only other player to score as many as 40 points in a single game was Benny Schall of Ft. Warren in 1943; he had 41 points against Capitol Life Insurance of Denver.

In the days of the AAU 50-team tournaments, as many as six regional quintets would be among the entries, including this 1948 Murphy-Mahoney Chevrolet team. Photo courtesy of the Denver Public Library, Western History Collection.

In the long run, the tournament was dominated by the teams from amateur basketball's organized leagues — first the Missouri Valley League then the American Basketball League, and finally the National Industrial Basketball League. Missouri Valley League teams won the first six Denver tournaments before dissolving in 1940. The ABL was dominated by the 66ers, who won all three of its championships in 1946, 1947 and 1948, as well as the AAU tournaments.

The NIBL began modestly in 1948, and went big-time in 1949 when it took over teams from the disbanded ABL. The NIBL stayed in business through the 1962 tournament, and from 1950 until its demise, one of its teams failed to win only in 1956 and 1957. The Buchan Bakers, who later joined the league, won in 1956 and the Air Force All-Stars took the in 1957 title.

Big company sponsorship cooled in the 1960s as black basketball players began to have more of an impact on the game. Phillips never did have a black player, Peoria had only Bob Boozer, and Wichita counted only home-grown Cleo Littleton. The Truckers pioneered with Horace Walker and Walt Mangham and later Dennis Boone, but the die had been cast. Peoria and Wichita ceased sponsorship after the 1960 tourney. A feeble attempt at a new industrial league was made in 1968 with Phillips, Akron, a team called the National Zip Codes from Milwaukee, and the Macomb,

The radio team of Fibber McGee 'n Molly, shown here with Mark Schreiber, left, sponsored an AAU team wearing green uniforms trimmed with shamrocks. Photo courtesy of Larry Zimmer.

Illinois AAU squad, but only Akron got as far as the semifinals.

The constant growth of professional basketball, which lured more and more players from the amateur ranks, had clouded the tournament's future for several years. Then the death blow was felt shortly after the 1968 event ended and Phillips 66 announced it would no longer field a team. Some 31 years of sponsorship were over. The new industrial league was gone, and so the Denver tournament died.

Indeed, the field had dropped from its 50-team high in the 1930s, 1940s and early 1950s to a mere 16 entries in the 1960s. The tournament lost money for the first time in 1967, and in 1968, no more than 2,200 fans attended any of the tournament sessions, including the finals, thanks to competition from the Denver Rockets of the American Basketball Association. In the National AAU tournament's last game, the Armed Forces All-Stars defeated Vaughn Realty of Spokane, 73-69, for the title.

Now AAU basketball in Denver has been gone for more than 20 years. To today's youngsters, its history probably means little. But to old-timers, the AAU's "Greatest Show on Earth" meant fans crowding into the unreserved front-row seats at the matinees, hanging over the balcony railings at the evening sessions, watching the Acer shoot those hooks in his duels with College Joe, booing the 66ers, heckling ol' Frankenstein, and living for the moments when the Luckett-Nixes and Poudre Valley Creameries would knock off the big guns.

Those were the days when all roads for hundreds of teams led to Denver, squads such as Panelshake Siding of Portland, the Leoti, Kansas Nighthawks, the Kable Kolts from Mount Morris, Illinois, the Allen-Bradleys from Milwaukee, Seattle's Alpine Dairy, the Eckers from Salt Lake City, the Idaho Simplots, the San Diego Dons, the Jamcos from Sioux City, Chicago's Jamaco Saints, M&O Cigars from Kansas City, Oakland's Blue 'n Gold and clubs out of Los Angeles, including Kirby's Shoes, Kelbo's Barbecue, Lockheed Aircraft, and a team wearing green uniforms trimmed with shamrocks sponsored by the radio comedy team of Fibber McGee 'n Molly.

For a week in late March, the AAU tournament was the only game in town, but like the dinosaurs that roamed Colorado in prehistoric times, the tournament, too, faded from existence. The players who once stood as tall as redwoods, both on the court and in the fancies of their followers unfortunately, didn't last as long.

***Opposite: Basketball today features players of all races. Photo courtesy of Rich Clarkson/*Sports Illustrated.**

***Bud Maloney** was a sportswriter with the* Rocky Mountain News *for 10 years from 1951 through 1961 and an avid follower of the National AAU basketball tournament for 14 years, from 1948 through 1961. He spent many, many afternoons and evenings at the old Denver Auditorium and at the Auditorium Arena during those years, and he wrote a history of the Denver tournaments in 1960.*

Reared in San Diego, California, Maloney came to Colorado in 1947 to enroll at the University of Denver. He graduated in 1951.

He now works for The San Diego Tribune.

WYOMING'S 1943 NCAA AND RED CROSS CHAMPS

FRANK HARAWAY

The "Pistol Pete" logo was most likely to have been used during the 1943 National Championship season.

A half-century ago, before airplanes became the usual mode of travel for athletic teams and everybody else, more easterners than not had the vague idea that westerners were largely involved in dodging behind trees and shooting Indians.

So it's not surprising that eastern sports culture received quite a shock in April of 1943 when a band of cowboys from the West, the Wyoming Cowboys, came to New York's hallowed Madison Square Garden to beat Georgetown, 46-34, for the NCAA basketball title. Two nights later, Wyoming whipped St. John's, the National Invitation Tournament winner, 52-47, in overtime, for the mythical national collegiate basketball championship.

To put all of this into perspective, one should remember that the nation at that time was much more concerned over the fact that Rommel's Africa Corps was eluding the Allies in Tunisia and American warplanes were engaging Japanese warships near the Solomon Islands. Sports, although recognized as an important prop to national morale at a time of grim international conflict, were vastly curtailed due to the military's needs for transportation and manpower.

Nonetheless, the Cowboys' accomplishments were cause for jubilation throughout the state. The team came home to wild celebrations and received carte blanche privileges in every eatery at a time when American families were scrounging for ways to get enough ration points to feed themselves.

In 1985, *Denver Post* sportswriter Kevin Simpson, in a full-page feature that detailed that unforgettable season with in-depth interviews of the surviving players, caught the mood of the moment.

"In the midst of World War II, it was a time of cataclysm and a time of joy, of innocence and coming of age," Simpson wrote. "All nine members of the championship team entered the military service in the weeks following that final game.

"The night of revelry in New York, the long [train] ride home, those were moments to be savored, yet the significance of the national title dawned slowly on the players, touching them at intervals through the ensuing decades. For the six surviving members of that championship season, the memories have slept mostly undisturbed, awakened intermittently by the death of the coach and three teammates."

Perhaps by coincidence, Wyoming's final two victims in that 31-2 season in 1943 – Georgetown and St. John's – remain two of the top powers in college basketball, while Wyoming in the 1980s has rekindled some of its past glory.

Architect of the 1943 championship team was a suave, but tough, basketball psychologist and disciplinarian, Everett Shelton. He had been lured to the Rocky Mountain region by William N. Haraway to coach the Denver Safeway team in National AAU basketball competition.

Haraway tried to induce the now legendary

Opposite: Kenny Sailors, the heart and soul of the 1943 championship team, was one of the first, if not the first, to perfect the jump shot.

The University of Wyoming team led by coach Ev Shelton receiving the championship trophy from Philip Badger, president of the NCAA at Madison Square Garden on March 30, 1943. Front row, left to right: Don Waite, Earl Ray, Jim Reese. Back row, left to right: Jim Collins, Floyd Volker, Milo Komenich, Ev Shelton, Lew Roney, Kenny Sailors, Jim Weir, Philip Badger.

Henry "Hank" Iba to coach the Denver Safeway team. Iba didn't want to give up his new Oklahoma State job but recommended that Haraway hire Shelton. "You couldn't obtain a better coach including myself," Iba said.

Haraway hired Shelton and in two seasons he gave Denver its first National AAU championship after the 1937-38 season. Shelton coached the Colorado Springs Antlers Hotel team in 1939 before moving on to Wyoming for 19 storied seasons.

This well-groomed, seemingly aloof, stoical man of dignity — in World War I, he had been a machine-gun sergeant at Chateau Thierry and Belleau Wood — was always in total control of his players.

"He instilled so much discipline on the court," said former player Moe Radovich, who later assisted Shelton and eventually became the Pokes' head coach. "You knew you'd had it if you made a mistake. If you got a technical, you just headed for the bench."

Bill Strannigan was a Rock Springs, Wyoming product who transferred to Wyoming from the University of Colorado and became an All-America player and later a successful coach. He called Shelton "defensively, the finest coach I have ever known. He did a lot of things that were ahead of his time, such as the five-man weave and movement without the ball."

Strannigan, one of Shelton's greatest players, graduated the year before the NCAA championship team, but Shelton took the rest of that squad and molded it into a title winner.

Of the nine players who made the trip to New York, all were from Wyoming, except 6'7" center Milo Komenich, who was from Gary, Indiana, and reserve guard Don Waite, who was from just across the state line in Scottsbluff, Nebraska. The seven Wyoming high school products were 5'11" forward Kenny Sailors from Laramie by way of Hillsdale, 6'6" forward Jim Weir from Green River, 6'3" guard Floyd Volker from Casper, and 6'3" guard Lew Roney from Powell, plus reserves Jimmy Collins from Laramie, Earl (Shadow) Ray from Casper and Jimmie Reese from Rock Springs.

"Can you imagine what Shelton did with 10 kids from Wyoming?" asks Wyoming native Curt Gowdy, an ordinary basketball player who went on to great fame as a sports broadcaster.

The diminutive Sailors was the heart and soul of that '43 Wyoming team, and sportswriters and broadcasters outdid themselves trying to find the right words to describe him. To some, he was a "whirling dervish." To others, a "dribbling fool," a "Houdini on the hardwood," a "ball-handling wizard." But more significantly, he was one of the first, if not *the* first, to employ the jump shot as it is known today.

Stanford's Hank Luisetti had wowed Garden fans five years earlier with his running, off-the-ear, one-handed shots from everywhere on the floor, but those were not strictly jump shots as we know them today.

"This Sailors can do everything with a basketball but tie a seaman's knot," wrote one New York sports editor, Joe Cummisky, after the Pokes' title win. "And, given time, and a chance to dribble two steps, he'd probably be able to do that. Sailors was the hand who held the S.S. Wyoming together when everybody was figuring Georgetown was in. It's enough to say that Sailors — also voted the most valuable player in the NCAA final as sort of an anti-climactic gesture — is quite a ballplayer."

Komenich was unique for centers of his day since his speed equaled that of many of his teammates. He also could score from the floor, as well as from under the basket. The big guy from Indiana was never better than in the Red Cross finale in New York, matched against the pride of the East, 6'9" Harry Boycoff of St. John's.

Here's how Cummisky described it: "I must be honest and admit that Big Boy Harry Boycoff met more than his match. . . . He tried to score, but couldn't. He tried all the tricks that had made him the best pivotman seen around here in years. Yet big Milo Komenich, who poured in 20 points [in Wyoming's 52-47 overtime win], made Boycoff look like he was still in high school. And that, more than anything else, was the reason St. John's was the runner-up to the first national champion in the history of collegiate basketball."

It should be noted that at that time, the NIT was every bit as prestigious — and maybe a bit more so — than the NCAA tourney. The win-

Coach Shelton was always in total control of his players, instilling harsh but effective discipline on the court. All photos and logo courtesy of the University of Wyoming Sports Information Office.

ners of the two competitions hadn't met in previous years to determine the "real" national college champion.

The third member of Wyoming's Big Three was burly Jim Weir, who teamed with Komenich to control the boards, while significantly contributing to the Pokes' scoring. Komenich had fouled out with a minute to play against St. John's, which then went on to tie the game and send it into overtime.

It was Weir who rode to the rescue in that extra period. He dropped in a one-hander for the first two of Wyoming's six points in the overtime, and with the Cowboys clinging to a 49-47 edge later on, he nailed another basket and converted a free throw to give the Cowboys their margin of victory.

Volker and Roney, the other members of Wyoming's starting five, didn't achieve the Big Three's fame, but they made valuable contributions and played good defense.

Collins would be known in today's parlance as the sixth man. Reese was Sailors' backup, and he possessed some of the same skills, especially as a dribbler and play-maker. His days in the limelight were to come later. Waite backed up Weir, and Ray — better known for his football skills — contributed a fiery spirit that became the team's trademark.

Due to the wartime curtailments, Wyoming's regular-season college play was limited to the revamped Mountain Five, comprised of the Cowboys, Colorado State University, Brigham Young University, the University of Utah and Utah State. The Cowboys swept a three-game playoff from BYU, the champions of the conference's western division, for the league title.

Wyoming's season — which followed three warmup victories over a strong Ft. Warren military team — started with an eastern trip in which the Cowboys won five of six, including a convincing romp over St. Francis in Madison Square Garden that gave eastern sportswriters their first glimpse of this upstart power from the West. Then came a pair of one-point midseason wins in a Denver infantile paralysis benefit series over the mighty Phillips 66ers, the acknowledged king-pins of amateur basketball.

Wyoming later entered the National AAU tourney in Denver and made it to the semi-finals before losing to the Denver Legion, the Pokes' only seasonal loss aside from a defeat at Duquesne.

After beating the University of Denver for third place in the AAU competition, the Cowboys turned their attention to the western regional NCAA playoffs in Kansas City, where they had to beat Oklahoma with Gerald Tucker, and Texas to qualify for the finals in New York.

The key to the Oklahoma game was the battle between Komenich and Tucker, and Shelton's game plan proved to be a key in Wyoming's 53-50 victory.

"We had an idea Tucker couldn't guard a big man and stay in the game, and we played it that way," Shelton said in explaining his defensive tactics which caused the Sooner star to foul out after 17 minutes with the Sooners leading 22-20. Komenich scored 15 of his game-leading points after Tucker's departure.

Texas' great forward, John Hargis, almost ended Wyoming's dreams in the western finale as he scored 29 points to lead the Longhorns to an early 26-13 lead. But calling on that intangible "something" which distinguishes champions from also-rans, the Cowboys worked their way back with a sensational rally and survived a seesaw finish to take a 58-54 win to New York and even greater glory.

Soon after that national championship victory, Sailors, Volker and Collins enlisted in the Marines going on to serve in the South Pacific. Reese and Waite joined the Naval Air Corps, but never saw combat duty. Ray went through officer's training school in Texas, but the war ended before he could be shipped overseas. Only Weir made it to the front lines. He suffered a shrapnel wound in the shoulder fighting the Germans, but returned home otherwise intact.

Prophetically enough, at a testimonial banquet in Cheyenne following the NCAA win, Wyoming's president J.L. Morrill, said, "The whole team will soon be in the armed services. Who doubts the victory there?"

Where are they today? Coach Everett Shelton: died of a heart attack in 1974; Jimmy Collins: killed in an auto crash in 1945; Milo Komenich: died of a heart attack in 1977; Jim Weir: died of a heart attack in 1977; Floyd Volker (70): sales manager for the Coors distributor in Casper; Lew Roney (66): retired teacher living in Laramie; Kenny Sailors (68): runs a guide service in Eakona, Alaska; Don Waite (64): runs a lumber company in Scottsbluff, Nebraska; Earl (Shadow) Ray (66): restaurant owner in Casper; Jimmie Reese (66): retired from GM's Buick division in Denver.

***Frank Haraway**, who has spent all but the first two months of his life in Colorado, has been an avid follower of sports in this area for more than 65 years, 44 of them as a sportswriter for* The Denver Post.

He estimates that he has attended more than 12,000 games, the majority of which he covered for The Post, *and he has watched countless more on television.*

Since retiring from The Post *on January 1, 1982, Haraway has remained active as a play-by-play producer for the Denver Broncos and the Denver Nuggets and as official scorer for the American Association's Denver Zephyrs. He also did correspondence work for* Sports Illustrated, The Sporting News *and other newspapers. Frank and his wife, June, are still familiar figures at nearly all sports events in Denver and in nearby college arenas.*

Haraway — who received a journalism degree from the University of Denver — enjoyed a long and close relationship with Everett Shelton, the coach of Wyoming's 1943 NCAA and Red Cross basketball champions, and he saw many of the Cowboys' 1943 games.

CINDERELLA TOOK THE TRAIN

JOHN MOONEY

The headline in *The Sporting News* on a mid-season story I had written announced, "Mile-High Country Sky-High on Towering Utes."

By 1944 standards, Utah's first NCAA champions were tall, if not towering. The starting five averaged 6′3″. Only Fred Sheffield, a sophomore, was a letterman. But Sheffield, the NCAA high jump champion, sprained an ankle in practice in Kansas City and was used sparingly in the NCAA.

The saga of 1944 was a fairy tale out of the Brothers Grimm. The military had taken over Utah's fieldhouse for barracks and the schedule included only three college opponents. The losses in a 17-3 regular season were to Dow Chemical, Fort Warren and Salt Lake Air Base.

The war was headline news then and Utah's departure for the National Invitational Tournament in Madison Square Garden was buried among the results of the state high school basketball tournament. Fittingly, none of Salt Lake City's three newspapers and none of the radio stations sent reporters or announcers with the team to New York due to newsprint and manpower shortages and transportation pressures.

Utah's schedule and lack of home court were disadvantages, but the Utes did have one advantage. Most college teams were bolstered by Navy V-12 or reserve programs, which limited the travel for those teams. But Utah's Sheffield was a pre-med student and not draftable, and Wat Misaka of Japanese ancestry was not eligible for military service. Indeed, the team averaged 18 1/2 years and no one was eligible for the draft.

Any advantage evaporated when the Utes faced Kentucky in the first round of the NIT in Madison Square Garden. Kentucky won, 46-38, and Utah's season apparently ended. But before the Utes could entrain for home, an opening came up in the Far West NCAA field when Arkansas was involved in a wreck and had to withdraw from the tournament.

Perry Sorensen, then sports information director for the Utes, remembers the acceptance vote.

"Because Utah didn't have a travel restriction like schools with V-12 or military personnel, the NCAA committee contacted Coach Vadal Peterson to see if Utah would be a last-minute substitute for the Razorbacks," Sorensen recalls.

"Coach Peterson called a team meeting for a vote and the Ute coach spoke against extending the season in favor of sightseeing in New York City. Also, the opening game against Missouri was only two nights away, which meant a long train ride and arrival just before the game.

"Utah had been the eighth and last team invited to the NIT, and now would be the eighth as a substitute in the NCAA. But the players, at a 2 a.m. meeting, voted unanimously to accept the bid."

Because of the lack of college opponents on its schedule and an unimpressive showing in the loss to Kentucky — plus the added train

Victory celebration in downtown Salt Lake City after the University of Utah returned from New York with the 1944 NCAA championship. Photo from They Were No. 1 *by Robert Stern.*

travel — Utah was a big underdog in both games in Kansas City. Even after defeating Missouri to gain the western finals, the Utes were expected to lose to Iowa State.

The team was held in such little regard that Sorensen later said that tournament director Reeves Peters had asked the Utes to let the Cyclones leave their luggage in Utah's hotel rooms, because the winner had to catch a midnight train to New York. As it turned out, the Utes ended up rushing to catch that sleeper after beating Iowa State, 40-31, to reach the championship round.

In the championship game at Madison Square Garden — where they had been beaten just 10 days earlier — the Utes upset Dartmouth on Herb Wilkinson's basket in overtime, 42-40. Utah then played St. John's, the NIT winner, in a Red Cross benefit and won, 43-36.

We tabbed them the "Blitz Kids" when they were dominating the area's basketball, but New Yorkers adopted them as "Destiny's Darlings."

Keith Brown, the graduate manager of Utah's athletic department, said by telephone after the game, "At the start of the game, most of the fans were for Dartmouth because it was an eastern team, but by the end, they were pulling for Utah. Arnie Ferrin was sensational. Dick Smuin, replacing the injured Sheffield, turned in a whale of a game."

The Utes returned home in triumph, and for a few days, shoved the war news into a secondary spot. Ferrin also added All-America honors to the Most Valuable Player trophy he'd won in New York.

The Utes were lucky to get a second chance to win a national championship in 1944, but their luck turned sour in their next two appearances in the Final Four, where they finished fourth both times. In 1961 and 1966, Utah was beaten in the semifinal games by the eventual NCAA champion, Cincinnati and Texas Western, respectively.

Utah may have been victimized by "expansion." In 1944, only eight teams started the competition in New York and Kansas City. In 1961 and 1966, 24 teams competed. In 1961, Utah lost in the semifinals to Cincinnati, 82-67, and then lost to St. Joseph's in four overtimes, 127-120, in the battle for third place. Later, it turned out that St. Joe's had to forfeit third place due to a gambling scandal.

Utah got to 1961's Final Four by beating the best in the west, Loyola of California, 91-75, and Arizona State, 88-80. Against Cincinnati —

Jerry Chambers, en route to becoming the 1966 NCAA tournament's most valuable player with a total of 143 points for the four tournament games, scored 24 points in the first half against Texas Western. Photo by Rich Clarkson. Except as noted, all photos and logo courtesy of University of Utah Sports Information Department.

Arnie Ferrin earned most valuable player designation as well as becoming an All-America athlete for his performance.

Utah's 1944 NCAA Champions, locally called the "Blitz Kids," were tagged as "Destiny's Darlings" by New Yorkers at the tournament.

which went on to beat Ohio State for the championship, 70-65 — the Utes were barely in the game as the Bearcats ran up a 17-12 advantage to a 29-16 edge. Utah never recovered even though Bill "The Hill" McGill poured in 25 points. When it was all over, Utah had finished with a 23-8 record.

Some called the 1966 NCAA tourney the "black and white" tournament because Kentucky and Duke weren't integrated. They fielded all-white teams, while Utah and Texas Western (now Texas-El Paso) had black players. That 1966 tournament go-round also was noteworthy because it was the only year from 1964 through 1973 that UCLA didn't win the title. The Bruins, in fact, didn't even make the Far West Regional field.

Playing on the UCLA court, the Utes swept through the western regional with an 83-74 victory over Pacific and a 70-64 win over Oregon State.

Jerry Chambers, en route to becoming the NCAA tournament's most valuable player, poured in 40 points as Utah walloped Pacific. Then, with Center George Fisher sidelined with a broken leg and Lyndon MacKay crippled with a tendon injury, the Utes broke fast against Oregon State with a 41-24 lead. That win allowed the WAC champions to breeze into the Final Four at Maryland.

But there, the breeze died. Texas Western, burned by Chambers' 24 points in the first half, tightened the defensive screws and handed the Utes an 85-78 whipping in the first round. Chambers scored only 14 points in the second half, while Bobby Joe Hill and Osten Artis added 18 and 22 points, respectively. Little Willie Worsley of Texas Western came off the bench to spark the defensive effort and put up 12 points for the Miners.

In the "kissing-your-sister" battle for third place, Utah lost to Duke, which had been ranked No. 2 behind Kentucky. The final score: 79-77 despite Chambers' 32 points, which gave him 143 points for the four tournament games.

The Blue Devils had held a 49-39 lead early in the second half, but Utah closed to 75-71 with four minutes left. MacKay, who hadn't been expected to play, dropped in two foul shots to cut Duke's margin to two. After trading baskets, Duke still led by two with less than a minute to go.

Chambers' basket offset a Duke free throw and Utah trailed, 78-77, with 35 seconds left. Chambers then fouled Jim Liccardo, and the Duke reserve missed both attempts at the line. Utah's Leonard Black drove the baseline and was fouled with seven seconds on the clock.

Duke tried to psyche out Black by calling two successive timeouts and the Ute reserve missed the front of the one-and-one opportunity. Duke added the final point on a free throw.

The Ute's haven't taken a late-night championship train ride for years now. But whenever we hear that whistle blowing somewhere far off in the Rockies, many of us sit back, remember when. Then cross our fingers and hope that one of these days, destiny will once again pull into Logan, holler "all aboard," and a bunch of gangly kids with basketballs tucked under their arms will take off for the ride of their lives.

John Mooney, *sports editor of* The Salt Lake Tribune, *is the dean of sportswriters in the Rocky Mountain area. A graduate of the University of Iowa, Mooney came to Salt Lake City in 1939 after a short stint on the sports staff of* The Chicago Tribune. *He became sports editor of* The Salt Lake Telegram *in 1941, and moved to* The Tribune *as sports editor in 1948.*

Mooney served as president of the Football Writers Association of America in 1969. He has received the annual Jake Wade Award (given by the College Sports Information Directors), the Bert McGrane Award (given by the Football Writers Association of America), and the meritorious service to journalism award from the University of Utah.

He is the only sportswriter in the Utah Sports Hall of Fame and the first active sportswriter to be voted an honorary football coach by the American Football Coaches Association.

Mooney has been on the Heisman, Lombardi and Davey O'Brien award selection committees and is a long-time member of the Honors Court, which selects National Football Foundation and Hall of Fame enshrinees..

He was married to his University of Iowa classmate, Betty Boiler, in 1937, and they have two children, Sharon and Joanne. Mrs. Mooney died in 1985.

UNIVERSITY OF COLORADO FINAL FOUR YEARS

FRED CASOTTI

The University of Colorado has reached the Final Four only once in eight NCAA tournament appearances because, more often than not, the Buffaloes have had the misfortune of running into a powerhouse.

Bebe Lee's 1955 squad is a good example. The team that breezed through what was then the Big Seven with an 11-1 mark sliced through the midwest regional with wins over Tulsa (69-59) and Bradley (93-61) behind Olympians-to-be Burdette Haldorson and Bob Jeangerard.

But waiting in Kansas City for the Buffs were Big Ten champ Iowa, the Tom Gola-led LaSalle Explorers and a San Francisco team that had come out of nowhere and into the tournament with a 24 game winning streak and 26-1 record.

The USF Dons were led by the intimidating Bill Russell, a junior who had established a regional reputation as a dominant force, especially on defense. Lee had been warned. His former teammate at Stanford during the Hank Luisetti era, Bob Burnett, had scouted the Dons extensively, and he delivered a report to the Buffs that focused on Russell and his very talented teammate, guard K.C. Jones. As Burnett noted, "You're not going to believe Russell until you see him. He does things I've never seen done before on a basketball floor."

Going into the tournament, the Buffs were seeded fourth. But they were a veteran team that had repeated as conference champion behind Haldorson, a deadly hook shot artist with either hand; Jeangerard, a ferocious defensive forward who could shoot, and the slick guard combination of Tom Harrold and Charlie Mock, who had played together since they were high school sophomores back in Muncie, Indiana. Then there were the power forwards, Mel Coffman and Jim Ranglos, who would make the all-tournament team, and two good backup guards, Bill Peterson and Mick Mansfield.

The Buffs' strategy against USF: Start Ranglos at center, move Haldorson to the corner, and have Harrold and Mock direct the deliberate attack that had become a CU trademark.

Disaster, however, struck moments before the opening tip. Harrold, cutting across the circle in a pre-game drill, slipped on a wet spot and badly sprained his ankle. Sophomore Mansfield started and played well, but the Colorado engine had blown a plug. Harrold tested the ankle soon after the tip but couldn't move, and he played only a few minutes.

At the outset, Lee's strategy seemed to work. Haldorson hit twice from outside, Russell had to move out to guard him, and the Buffs led 10-6 after six minutes. Then Russell began to display his hidden offensive talents. He scored five straight points, evening up the game until the half's closing seconds when San Francisco's deadly mid-court press produced two turnovers, two baskets and a 25-19 lead at the intermission.

The Dons widened their margin to 31-19 at

Colorado's Jim Ranglos started at center against San Francisco and earned a spot on the All-Final Four team.

Colorado's 1969 Final Four Squad. Front row: Trainer Jack Rockwell, Tom Harrold, Will Walter, Bob Helzer, George Red-Hair, Byron Bennett, Dave Mowbray, Coach H.B. Lee. Middle row: Manager John Roberts, Gordon Johnson, Sammy Morrison, Charlie Mock, Jamie Grant, Bill Peterson, Bob Decker, Jim Grant, Jim Cadle, Bob Yardley, Assistant Gerry Ellyson. Back row: Assistant Bill Tom, Mel Cofman, Jim Ranglos, Bob Jeangerard, Burdette Haldorson, Frank Wilcox, George Hannah, Jim Jochems, Lee Hayward, Mick Mansfield, Jerry Spicer.

the start of the second half, and Colorado's faint chances evaporated when Haldorson fouled out only six minutes into the period.

The rest of the game became a one-man show as Russell amazed the crowd with his rim-rattling jams including a reverse, over-the-head dunk. He finished with a game-high 24 points and the Dons won, 62-50.

The next night, the Buffs destroyed Iowa, 75-54, behind Ranglos' 18 points, and San Francisco crushed LaSalle for the title.

Colorado's first appearance in the NCAA tourney in 1940 came a week after the Buffs had won the National Invitational Tournament title. Coached by Frosty Cox and led by the NIT's most valuable player, Bob Doll, who had sparked CU to Madison Square Garden wins over DePaul and Duquesne, the Buffaloes were favored to win the western regional, but fell to Southern California, 38-32. The next night, they lost to Rice in overtime, 60-56.

In 1942, Cox's men again entered the tournament impressively, ranked as the nation's No. 1 team after running up a 16-1 regular season record.

The first round foe was Cox's alma mater, Kansas, where he had been an outstanding guard under Phog Allen. Now, the two men were opponents. Adding to the pre-game fuel was the fact that Cox had seven Kansans on CU's roster. The Buffs got a big night from Pete McCloud, who popped in 19 points to pace CU past the Jayhawks, 46-44. But the next night, Stanford held McCloud to three points and Colorado fell, 46-35.

Cox, who had built CU into a national power after taking over in 1936, got one more shot at the NCAA's brass ring after he assembled a group of Navy trainees and youngsters who went 12-4 in 1946.

However, the Buffs weren't up to the task and lost the tournament opener, 50-44, to California. Colorado turned around and hammered Baylor, 59-44, in the consolation game. One of the youngsters on that team was rising backcourt star Sox Walseth who would, in

Guard Charlie Mock (5) was one of CU's key ballhandlers. Except as noted, all photos courtesy of Fred Casotti.

Bill Marolt, University of Colorado Athletic Director, and Bill Daniels hosted the NCAA Division I Mens Basketball Committee before the 1989 West Regional Championship game in Denver. Photo courtesy of Bob Sprenger.

1962, become the first and only man to play for and later coach CU in NCAA competition.

Lee's 1954 crew tied Kansas for the Big Seven title with a furious finish that saw the Buffaloes go 11-2 after losing their first six games. But that string ran out in the regionals at Stillwater, Oklahoma, as first Bradley and then Rice buried the Buffs by scores of 76-64 and 78-55, respectively. Worth noting is the fact that Bradley guard Bob Carney hit 23 of 26 free throws en route to a 37-point night to overshadow fine games by Mock and Harrold who scored 17 and 13, respectively.

Walseth, who succeeded Lee in 1956, led the Buffs to the NCAA tourney in 1962 and 1963. A sound, innovative leader, just as Cox had been, Walseth had the poor fortune to be in the same regional bracket as powerhouse Cincinnati, which had barely missed winning two straight national championships.

Led by All-America forward Ken Charlton, spidery center Jim Davis and silky Wilky Gilmore, the Buffs opened with a 67-60 win over Tulsa. But CU was outgunned by Cincinnati's bigger, stronger Bearcats, 73-46. A year later, with Charlton burning the nets, the Buffs beat Oklahoma City, 78-72, and then took Cincinnati to the wire before bowing, 67-60. Charlton scored 49 points in the two games.

Like his mentor, Walseth had a third shot at the NCAA crown in 1969 with what was probably his finest team. Led by Cliff Meely — generally regarded as CU's best cager ever — the Buffs wrapped up Walseth's third Big Eight title. But despite Meely's 32 points, the Buffs were upset by rival Colorado State, 64-56, as the Rams placed four scorers in double figures. The Buffs then had to settle for the consolation of scoring the most points by a CU team in NCAA play as they outraced Texas A&M, 97-82, the next night.

Today, CU's record in eight NCAA tournament appearances stands at 8 wins, 10 losses. The breakdown shows Cox at 2-4 in three tourneys, Lee 3-3 in two NCAAs and Walseth 3-3 in three appearances.

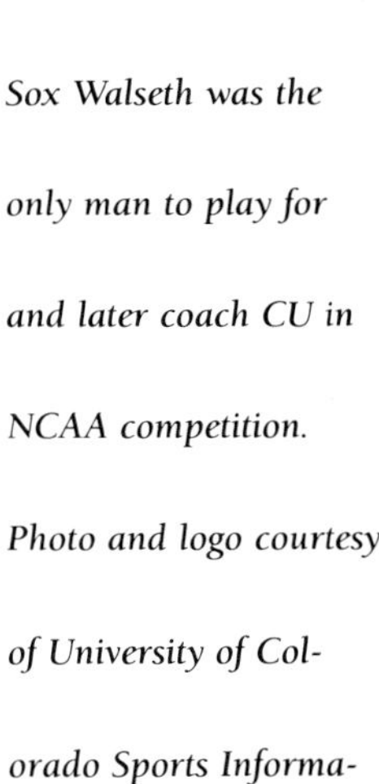

Sox Walseth was the only man to play for and later coach CU in NCAA competition. Photo and logo courtesy of University of Colorado Sports Information Department.

Fred Casotti, *a native of Fraser, Iowa, came to the University of Colorado as a student in 1947. After a three-year stint as a sportswriter in Council Bluffs, Iowa, he returned to Boulder to stay in 1952. He was sports information director at CU from 1952 to 1967, assistant athletic director from 1968 to 1972, and associate athletic director from 1973 to 1985.*

He has been serving as a special assistant to athletic director Bill Marolt since his retirement.

L A D Y B U F F S

JUNE HARAWAY

A standing-room only crowd of 11,199 for a women's basketball game in Colorado?

Amazing as it sounds, that's what happened on March 18, 1989, when the University of Colorado Lady Buffs hosted the University of Nevada-Las Vegas in their first-ever NCAA tournament home game at the CU Events Center in Boulder.

The Lady Buffs couldn't deliver a victory for the wildly enthusiastic crowd, losing 84-74. But the fact that CU didn't make it over the top didn't detract from the team's remarkable, season-long deeds:

— A 14-0 Big Eight record and the conference title, plus three more victories in the post-season tournament.

— A 20-game winning streak before the loss to UNLV, just one game off the longest athletic winning streak in CU history, set by the football team from 1908 to 1912.

— A 27-4 season won-lost record.

— A No. 9 ranking in the final Associated Press women's basketball poll.

Far overshadowing these statistical accomplishments, however, was the status the team brought to women's basketball at CU and throughout the region.

To grasp this fully, one must go back to the humble beginnings of women's basketball, which got its impetus from Title 9 requirements instituted in the 1970s. The Lady Buffs played their first season in 1974-75 under coach Carol Hochsprung, winning only two of 11 games in front of crowds that usually included only a few fans and some players' relatives and friends.

Three seasons under coach Jerry Zancanelli produced a 40-38 record before the school imported Rene Portland, who advanced the program by posting 22-9 and 18-11 records before leaving.

Sox Walseth, the winningest men's basketball coach in CU history, came out of retirement in 1980 to coach the women's team. He proved to be immensely popular with the girls, and his teams compiled records of 28-5 (most wins in a season in CU history), 28-8 and 21-8 before he turned things over to Ceal Barry.

By this time, the Lady Buffs had moved from the Intermountain Conference to the Big Eight. It took Barry two seasons of rebuilding to get the program back on the track that led to the remarkable 1988-89 season.

The story of this team must begin with the recruitment of the class led by Bridget Turner, Tracy Tripp, Crystal Ford and Gretchen DeWitte.

All four wound up among the top ten career Lady Buff scoring leaders, with Turner topping out at 1,599 points, second to CU record holder Lisa VanGoor's 2,067. Tripp was close behind Turner with 1,574 career points.

"What they did was establish a standard," says Barry. "They led us to two consecutive NCAA tournament appearances and to the Big Eight championship. So even though their careers here are over, their presence will still be

Head Coach Ceal Barry, the Big Eight's Coach of the Year, guided the Lady Buffs to their best season ever.

felt because of the tradition they set for future players."

In addition to her scoring, Turner, the Big Eight Player of the Year, was the team's playmaker and leader. Tripp was a good outside shooter who became adept at passing. Ford was an effective post player, and DeWitte was an offensive threat from the perimeter.

Little Annan "Spud" Wilson contributed some remarkable three-point shooting. Rosland Starks rebounded well as a starter, and Benita Martin and Cheryl Woodford added bench strength.

"They learned to complement, not counter, each other," Barry says. "The seniors were my kind of players who fit into our deliberate half-court style. We've had better athletes come and go, but there haven't been many who played smarter than they did."

No mention of the 1988-89 season would be complete without mention of CU's 61-60 midseason conquest of perennial women's basketball power Louisiana Tech, which finished No. 3 in the final AP rankings. The win provided the first real evidence of the emerging interest in women's basketball at CU as 5,767 cheered the Lady Buffs' victory.

1988-89 University of Colorado Lady Buffs Basketball Team. Front row, left to right: Annan Wilson, Bridget Turner, Benita Martin, Deborah Jacobson and Tracy Tripp. Back row, left to right: Jen Tubergen, Rosland Starks, Cheryl Woodford, Crystal Ford, Sherrice King, Gretchen DeWitte and Lisa Weatherspoon.

Senior point guard Bridget Turner led the 9th-ranked Lady Buffs to a first place finish in the Big Eight Conference and a berth in the NCAA tournament.

Annan "Spud" Wilson is Colorado's lone returning starter for the 1989-90 season. All Lady Buffs photos and logo courtesy of University of Colorado Sports Information Office.

Their 1988-89 accomplishments produced two important aftereffects. First, Barry received her first coaching contract at CU, a three-year pact beginning with the 1989-90 season. Second, women's Big Eight games, which usually had been played before men's games, are now single-game attractions. Any way you look at it, women's basketball in Colorado came of age in 1988 and 1989 thanks to the Lady Buffs.

A Denver Post sports columnist once described **June Haraway** *as "superfan," a description most appropos. She attended countless baseball, football and basketball games as well as golf tournaments, in high school and young adulthood.*

She also served as a scout for the San Francisco Giants and once sponsored a semi-pro baseball team for collegiate players in the summertime.

After her marriage to Denver Post sportswriter Frank Haraway, she accompanied him on practically all of his assignments and has continued to do so since his retirement.

June has followed the University of Colorado Lady Buffs since their birth and has seen nearly all of their home games.

DENVER - 1912
THE REAL REASON THEY CALLED HER "THE UNSINKABLE" MOLLY BROWN
THUNK
DADGUM, MOLLY! THAT'S 500 IN A ROW YOU'VE MISSED!
Rocky Mountain News

REGIONAL BASKETBALL ON RADIO AND TV

LARRY ZIMMER

This is the first time that Denver has hosted the NCAA Final Four Championships, but it's not the first time a championship tournament has received extensive broadcast coverage in the Mile High City.

Indeed, the National AAU Tournament was a fixture here for years. At least four local radio stations carried games, often from early morning to midnight.

Mark Schreiber was the big name in broadcasting through the 1930s and 1940s in the Rockies, and he remained active on the Colorado broadcast scene into the 1960s. Schreiber, who now lives in Santa Rosa, California, recalls that he did his first basketball broadcast in the late 1930s probably on KVOD or KFEL. There was great interest in the Denver Nuggets, who played in the Missouri Valley AAU League. The team, operated by a group of local businessmen, won the National AAU Tournament in its first year, which led to the first basketball broadcast.

KMYR went on the air in early 1941 and became Denver's dominant sports voice. Schreiber showed up and did the play-by-play on the first college game in the Denver market — a contest involving the Wyoming Cowboys. Broadcasting the game and finding sponsors was the easy part; getting there was the trick. During World War II, gasoline was rationed and Schreiber says the fans passed the hat in the stands to collect enough gasoline stamps so he could make the trip to Laramie.

Starr Yelland, Mark Schreiber and Bill Day broadcast from courtside, about 1945.

Schreiber followed the Cowboys to the NCAA championship and remembers the thrill of broadcasting the finals in the old Madison Square Garden. He had to do some fast talking with the Garden's major domo, Ned Irish, who couldn't believe that a broadcaster from Denver was going to do the games "live." But Schreiber worked it out somehow and more Rocky Mountain broadcast history was made.

In the post-war years, Schreiber — who sold most of the advertising spots himself, often trading time for a suit or a pair of shoes — announced selected college games on KMYR and often talked coaches into sitting in on the broadcasts. Two of his more legendary guests were Henry Iba of Oklahoma A&M and Dr. Forrest "Phog" Allen of Kansas.

Radio was on its way to becoming a big part of the Denver basketball scene and Schreiber expanded his coverage to include high school games. KOA and KLZ joined the sports bandwagon, covering the popular AAU tournament, and Schreiber's broadcast partners soon included KOA news director Bill Day and Starr

Yelland, who would become a major sports personality in the Rockies for three decades.

In the 1950s, Schreiber began to devote more time to his burgeoning advertising business, but he still did selected broadcasts.

In the meantime, Bill Reed (who died in July, 1989) and Fred Leo were becoming friendly broadcast competitors. Reed was the voice of the Denver Bears baseball team for 15 years, but he also did quite a bit of basketball broadcasting on KMYR and KFEL, which would become KIMN.

Leo's first broadcast in Denver was done for a Peoria, Illinois, station when he covered the Peoria Caterpillars in an AAU tournament. Leo moved to Denver in 1952 and became KMYR's primary broadcaster in 1953. Schreiber joined Leo on the first telecast of a Colorado Buffaloes game from old Balch Field House in Boulder against Kansas and Wilt Chamberlain. The game was produced by KBTV-Channel 9, and Leo and Schreiber remember that viewers not only saw the action, but got a good dose of the CU pep band since the announcers' booth was right above its stand. Chamberlain, by the way, got upset with Sox Walseth's zone defense, quit shooting, and ended up with only 6 points.

Bill Reed and Gene Amole did the first professional basketball game ever broadcast in Denver. Reed, who died in July, 1989, will be remembered for his avid interest in sports which was conveyed in all of his broadcasts.

Leo later turned his full energy to television as sports anchor on KWGN-Channel 2, where he handled high school basketball tournament telecasts in the late 1950s. Through the 1960s, Leo was a fixture behind the radio microphone, broadcasting about 150 high school, college and AAU games a season. At tournament time, he did the Catholic schools tournament, the public schools tournament and the AAU tournament on successive weekends, sometimes covering four games a day.

He recalls that one of the most listened-to games was the final contest of the 1955 AAU Tournament between the Phillips 66ers and the Luckett-Nix team of Boulder. The Colorado Buffaloes finished third in the NCAA tournament that season and Luckett-Nix had five CU seniors anchor its squad — Burdette Haldorson, Bob Jeangerard, Tommy Harrold, Charlie Mock and Bob Yardley. However, they lost the title game, 66-64, on a last-second shot by the 66ers' Jim Walsh.

Later, the Denver-Chicago Truckers became the city's major team in the old National Industrial Basketball League, and Leo did the games, including the 1961 championship season.

Many still remember the popular broadcast team of Bill Reed and Gene Amole, who combined to do all the University of Denver games in 1954 and 1955. The Pioneer games were replaced in 1956 by a schedule of Colorado, Colorado State, Regis College and Air Force Academy contests, and Reed did a full season of Colorado State games, as well.

Reed remembered one interesting trip in which he broadcast CU-Northwestern in Evanston, Illinois; Regis-Dayton in Dayton; CU-Cincinnati on the Bearcats' home floor; and Regis-University of Detroit in the Motor City on four consecutive nights just before Christmas. When it finally was time to head back to Colorado, snow was falling and it was touch-and-go whether Reed would get out of the snowbound Detroit airport in time to return to Denver before Santa Claus arrived.

"I remember the wait, because the famous labor leader, Jimmy Hoffa, was also waiting for a flight," he recalled. "We did make it home, eventually, for Christmas."

Some still remember Reed's broadcasts of the NBA Nuggets in 1949-50 when the team won only 11 games. Reed and Amole did the home games from the DU field house on KMYR, while most of the road games were recreated in the studio.

"They were fun," Reed said. "The telegrapher at the game would tell you who scored the basket and where the shot came from, and we just made up the rest. You could get very dramatic and creative as long as you had the right guy scoring the basket."

Reed remembered one time that didn't work.

"The team was playing back east and one of the bench warmers was scoring all the points," he said. "The leading scorer's name had not been mentioned on the ticker. We queried the telegrapher and asked him to doublecheck what he was sending.

"The bench warmer continued to have a great game, so Gene and I made a big deal out of it, assuming the star was sick. He scored 20 points, a lot in those days. Well, it turns out the points were really scored by the star. He had changed uniforms and was wearing the bench warmer's number."

Then there were times when wrong names would creep into the broadcasts on purpose! Amole recalls when he and Reed were unhappy about having to do a game on Christmas night, so they inserted players named "Donner" and "Blitzen" into the lineup. Reed could get away with stunts like that since he was quite the celebrity. He also was a fastidious dresser known to wear two or three different suits in a single day. One colleague remembers Reed buying 27 pairs of shoes during one visit to a shoe store. At basketball games, however, he couldn't practice his baseball custom of removing his trousers in the booth so they could hang on a hanger to keep their crease.

Bob Martin, now the dean of active Denver sportscasters, joined KMYR in the 1950s. He and Bob Rubin later were partners at KMOR in Littleton, doing a heavy schedule of high school and college basketball games.

By the mid-1960s, KMYR had become KDEN, and KLZ, KTLN and KOA were doing more sports. Spencer Haywood joined the Denver Rockets of the old American Basketball Association and the team became a contender as Martin did the play-by-play on KTLN and the playoffs on television. He joined KOA in 1970 and the Rockets' broadcasts went with him. By the end of the 1974 season, the minor league Denver Spurs seemed to be headed to the National Hockey League, so KOA cast its lot with hockey. In the meantime, the Rockets

Fred Leo's first broadcast in Denver was done for a Peoria, Illinois, station when he covered the Peoria Caterpillars in an AAU tournament. Leo moved to Denver in 1952 and continued broadcasting as many as 150 high school, college and AAU games a season.

Gene Amole worked with Bill Reed to broadcast all the NBA Nuggets basketball games, doing the home games from the DU field house, while most of the road games were recreated in the studio.

became the Nuggets and joined the National Basketball Association, while the Spurs joined the World Hockey Association and went bankrupt.

The Nuggets eventually returned to KOA after a two-year stint on KHOW, where Mike Wolfe manned the microphone during the first year and Al Albert, the former voice of the New York Nets, handled broadcast chores the second year. Albert continued to do the broadcasts on KOA until he moved back to New York. Bill Howard, who had been the voice of the Utah Stars, filled in for a few games and then gave way to Jeff Kingery, who is still the Nuggets' play-by-play voice on KOA.

Bob Martin, now the dean of active Denver sportscasters joined KMYR in the 1950s. Photo by Howard Oda. Except as noted, all photos courtesy of Larry Zimmer.

Since the 1970s, college basketball has taken a back seat in Denver. KOA did CU games in the late 1970s and early 1980s unless there was a Nuggets conflict. KHOW got the CU football/basketball package in 1982 and took Wayne Larribee's Sports Network feed for two years. The games moved to KNUS the next year, but since then, the Buffs haven't been on Denver radio on a regular basis.

I've been doing the broadcasts for CU since 1985, working with Rusty Schaffer on KBOL in Boulder, which has been the voice of Buffs basketball since 1947. Before us, the station's roster of announcers has included Don Roper, Pete Hansson and Jim Kithcart.

In Ft. Collins, CSU games have been on KCOL where Bill Hansson and Al Trask have been the principal broadcasters. Jack Finlayson was the long-time voice of the Air Force Falcons on KVOR in Colorado Springs, but the Academy's broadcasts have never consistently cracked the Denver market.

The broadcasting fixture for Wyoming basketball in the Laramie-Cheyenne market is Larry Birleffi, a longtime Curt Gowdy associate. Gene Benson also broadcast the Cowboys for a number of years before taking over the Air Force network and later adding the Colorado State games.

Even though college basketball doesn't have a radio foothold in Denver — and the network affiliates often relegate local teams to the wee hours — cable television has given the games exposure thanks to United Cable's increasingly ambitious schedule of CU and CSU games.

Jeff Kingery is now the play-by-play voice on KOA for all of the Nuggets' games. Photo courtesy of KOA Radio.

When NBC had college basketball exclusively, Big 8 and Western Athletic Conference games were regularly televised on Saturday afternoons in Denver. Jay Randolph and Gary Thompson handled the Big 8 games for several years, and I joined Bill Strannigan on the WAC telecasts in 1980, succeeding Connie Alexander of Albuquerque.

Rusty Schaffer, working with Larry Zimmer, has broadcast the University of Colorado Buffs basketball games since 1985 on KBOL, Boulder. Photo courtesy of Rusty Schaffer.

I remember once when Strannigan became ill the day before one of our telecasts in Laramie. On Friday night, producer Dick Siley called Irv Brown at the halftime of a University of New Mexico game he was refereeing in Albuquerque to see if Brown could get to Laramie the next day. Brown made it in time for the telecast and with that, started down the road of what has become a successful broadcast career.

Doing games with a former official who also was the league's supervisor of officials had dramatic moments. Coaches who felt victimized by bad calls would turn and glare at us. San Diego State's Smoky Gaines once came to our broadcast site to argue a call with Irv while we were trying to announce the game. Then there was the game at Air Force when I felt someone breathing heavily over my shoulder. It was UTEP's Don Haskins demanding that we show him a replay of a call he disagreed with.

Basketball broadcasting in the Rockies has been colorful, but now the only game in Denver focuses on the professional Nuggets. The enthusiasm for college basketball is there; all the fans need is a winner. But while Colorado State's program is on the upswing and CU's program is on the mend, it's doubtful that the airwaves will ever be as full of basketball as they were in the golden days that stretched from 1950 to 1970.

***Larry Zimmer** grew up in football-mad Baton Rouge, Louisiana and got his journalism degree at the University of Missouri, when he started his broadcasting career as the color announcer on Missouri Tiger games during the Sparky Stalcup era. He also did local high school games.*

Zimmer moved to Ann Arbor, Michigan in 1966, where he was the voice of Michigan Wolverine football and basketball on WAAM. He came to Denver's KOA in 1971.

He and Bob Martin have done the Denver Broncos' broadcasts since 1971, and today, they are the National Football League's senior broadcast team. Zimmer also has been the play-by-play voice of University of Colorado football since 1971, save for the three years when he handled Colorado State University football broadcasts on KOA. He also broadcast the Denver Rockets of the old American Basketball Association and has handled the ABA and play-by-play chores of the Western Athletic Conference regional basketball telecasts.

Zimmer has announced many NCAA tournament games for NCAA Productions and ESPN, including the Alabama-North Carolina State regional semifinal in Denver in 1985.

THE FINAL FOUR AND THE NATIONAL MEDIA

BUDDY MARTIN

Magazines courtesy of Boulder Public Library. Photo by Warren Blanc, the Image Maker. Reproduced with permission.

We didn't call it the Final Four when I first started working in the sports department back in the early 1960s. It was known as the NCAA Basketball Finals and it drew about the same amount of attention from the national media as, oh, say Wimbledon tennis, the America's Cup and the Westminster Dog Show put together.

That was BJW (before John Wooden) put Westwood on the map. College basketball was still a regional delight and despite its enormous popularity in places like Indiana, Kentucky, North Carolina, New York City, Kansas and Chicago, the game still lacked major national appeal.

In some areas of the United States, college basketball was nothing more than an adjunct of the football program and, in some cases, the sport was coached by a football assistant. Fewer than half the newspapers sent staff representatives to cover the NCAA basketball finals back then.

The big ticket items for sports editors were the World Series; the NFL or AFL Championship games in the pre-Super Bowl days; the Rose, Orange, Sugar and Cotton bowls; the Masters Tournament and US Open; and maybe the Kentucky Derby. And, of course, every four years, the Olympics.

Television had already skyrocketed sports like golf and pro football into national prominence, but college basketball lacked continuity from season to season. And despite magnificent scoring performances by players such as Elgin Baylor of Seattle in 1958, Jerry West of West Virginia in 1959, and Oscar Robertson of Cincinnati in 1960, college basketball was not a sport embraced by network TV audiences.

As TV technology improved — did you ever try to find the basketball on a 12-inch black-and-white screen? — and the Information Age dawned on America, however, the world soon found out about the Wizard of Westwood and his UCLA dynasty. It was Wooden who helped introduce the public to the high drama of college basketball in living color.

Nothing quite caught the public's attention like the Wooden Era, which lasted for a dozen years. That grandfatherly figure with the rumpled trousers and the genteel manner was in our living rooms from 1964 to 1975 more than Ozzie and Harriett were in the 1950s.

Ten times out of 12, the Bruins won national championships, with only Texas-El Paso's upset of Kentucky in 1966 and North Carolina State's defeat of Marquette in 1974 breaking what would have been a dozen straight. There was an aura of suspense about UCLA's dominance and its ability to fight off challengers as the Bruins kept turning over new personnel without losing their near-permanent grip on the trophy.

Lew Alcindor, who later became Kareem Abdul-Jabbar, was a symbol of UCLA's supremacy as the gifted center was named the tournament's most outstanding player three

Lew Alcindor, who later became Kareem Abdul-Jabbar, was a symbol of UCLA's basketball supremacy, having been named the tournament's most valuable player three consecutive times.

UCLA coach John Wooden helped introduce the public to the high drama of college basketball.

The public and media took to Alcindor and UCLA, which used the Final Four as its Great White Way.

consecutive times. As a barometer of UCLA's balance, Alcindor didn't lead the tournament in scoring any of those three years. In 1967 and 1968, Elvin Hayes of Houston averaged 25.6 and 33.4 points, respectively; in 1969 it was Rick Mount of Purdue with a 30.5 per-game average.

Although nobody guessed that Alcindor would someday replace Wilt Chamberlain as pro basketball's most prolific scorer, there were some people who recognized his awesome talent during his college days. Former Denver Nuggets star and Kentucky Wildcat captain Dan Issel remembered seeing Alcindor in Louisville in 1967 when UCLA beat Dayton for the title.

"I had never seen anything like him in my life," Issel recalls, "and his graceful moves were fascinating." To this day, Issel still regards Abdul-Jabbar as "the greatest player of all time."

The public and media took to Alcindor and UCLA, which used the Final Four as its Great White Way, and Bruin-haters were spawned in the same fashion as Yankee-haters were in the 1950s.

In 1968, UCLA's 47-game winning streak was on the line when Wooden's troops traveled to Houston to play before more than 50,000 fans in the Astrodome. The Cougars, behind Elvin Hayes' shooting, knocked off the Bruins 71-69, and it was this setting that probably convinced the NCAA that college basketball was something more than a break between college football seasons.

*Big Bill Walton helped continue the Bruin's winning years. All photos courtesy of Rich Clarkson/*Sports Illustrated.

The first Final Four I covered was 1970 at College Park, Maryland, the year after Alcindor graduated. As a sports columnist in Florida, I was tracking Jacksonville University, which surprised everyone by making it to the championship game before losing to the Bruins, 80-69.

Back then, the title game was played on Saturdays, not Mondays, and the NCAA had not yet begun holding the tournament in super-structures such as the Superdome and Kingdome. Tickets, however, were not nearly so scarce, and while the games were sellouts, scalping was not necessarily a profitable venture.

I wish I could say I had projected the rosy future of the Final Four, but, honestly, I never had any idea it would grow so rapidly in stature. I found my first Final Four exciting up close, but then, what young sportswriter covering a state team at that level wouldn't?

There was almost no way to know that in the 1980s the Final Four would become one of America's top showcases. Today, only the World Series and perhaps the Super Bowl outrank the Final Four each year in the media's pecking order.

As late as the early 1970s, however, the Final Four event still wasn't commanding the media's full respect in many markets. Indeed, nobody from my paper, *The St. Petersburg Times*, covered the NCAA Finals, even though it had dispatched a columnist to Munich for the 1972 Olympics. Today, every major newspaper in America sends at least one sports staffer to the Final Four — many send two or more — and the NCAA must limit the press credentials it issues.

Each year, it seems, the Final Four has grown in popularity. Probably no other tournament heightened the interest more than the 1979 go-round in Salt Lake City when Michigan State's Earvin "Magic" Johnson and Indiana State's Larry Bird introduced the college crowd to Showtime.

Great players such as Isiah Thomas (Indiana, 1981), James Worthy (North Carolina, 1982), Akeem Olajuwon (Houston, 1983) and Patrick Ewing (Georgetown, 1984) elevated the prominence of the Final Four in the past decade.

College basketball, in general, has enjoyed tremendous growth in the 1980s, and one reason is the Final Four's glamorous staging. Certainly, the central characters change every few years, so it can't be Bobby Knight's volatile temper, Jim Valvano's eccentric personality or Dean Smith's suits that keep attracting attention.

So what is it?

I and others contend that it's the hoopla of the college sport which makes it so appealing — the same hoopla that goes begging in the NBA. For example, Irv Brown, the Denver radio personality who refereed six times in the Final Four, says, "It's my favorite event. There is still nothing quite like that first day when all four teams are participating, the bands and the cheerleaders are going and the crowd is all excited. Nothing like it."

Well, nothing like it as far as Brown knows. Of course, he's never been to Madison Square Garden for the finals of the Westminster Dog Show.

Wilton Francis "Buddy" Martin II, *a long-time* Denver Post *sports columnist, author and radio commentator, is about to enter his fourth decade as a sports journalist.*

At age 20, Martin was named sports editor of his hometown newspaper, the Ocala, Florida Star-Banner, *while on temporary leave from the University of Florida.*

Since then, he has been sports editor of the Today *newspaper in Brevard County, Florida; New York City sports columnist for Gannett News Service; sports editor and features editor of the* St. Petersburg, Florida Times; *executive sports editor of* The New York Daily News, *and Assistant Managing Editor/Sports of* The Denver Post.

He also has been a sportswriter at The Nashville Tennessean, Atlanta Constitution, *and* Jacksonville Journal, *as well as a staff writer in the Miami bureau of United Press International. Martin is the father of two daughters and a son. In September, 1989, he accepted a position with the* Florida Times Union *in Jacksonville, where he also plans to do radio and TV assignments. Martin recently finished his third book,* Passing Through, *the autobiography of former Pittsburgh Steeler quarterback Terry Bradshaw.*

CBS' ROLE IN THE FINAL FOUR

JIM NANTZ

It's called "March Madness" and not without good reason.

In the past decade, we've all watched and participated as the Final Four has grown in scope and stature into one of the premier events in all of sports, taking its place on every fan's calendar with the Super Bowl, the World Series and horse racing's Triple Crown.

At CBS Sports, we have more than a passing interest in this growth. The Final Four is the cornerstone of our first-quarter programming. Since 1982, when we first televised the tournament, our commitment has grown to the point that it now includes three weekends of coverage and six prime-time games. This year, CBS will air 31 games, and the total audience will make the NCAA tournament the most-viewed event in American sports.

As we prepare for our biggest effort ever here in Denver, we can't help but wonder about the magical moments we will soon come to forever associate with college basketball's Rocky Mountain high.

Looking back, certain cities have become synonymous with modern day *classics*. In New Orleans, a freshman named Michael Jordan helped North Carolina stun the powerful Georgetown Hoyas.

In Albuquerque, Jim Valvano's Cardiac Kids broke the hearts of Houston's Phi Slamma Jamma fraternity. In Lexington, the real thoroughbreds were long shots from Villanova who upset Georgetown in a photo finish. And in Kansas City, Danny Manning and his Kansas Jayhawks celebrated the Final Four's 50th anniversary with a golden performance against favorite Oklahoma.

The Rockies last hosted the Final Four a decade ago, when Salt Lake City was the setting for a fabulous matchup between Larry Bird of Indiana State and Earvin "Magic" Johnson of Michigan State — a confrontation that was the springboard for two of the most exciting careers in basketball history.

It has already been decreed that Denver's McNichols Sports Arena will be the last of the "smaller" halls to host a Final Four tournament. That leaves us feeling nostalgic even before it begins here because that unique intimacy can never be equalled in a domed stadium.

But that will not subtract from our CBS Sports effort. We will marshal the talents of more than one-hundred specialists, from executive producer Ted Shaker, producer Bob Dekas and director Bob Fishman in the truck to Brent Musburger and Billy Packer at courtside.

The real scramble, of course, begins three weeks before the tournament when we try to figure out the 64 teams that will be invited before they're officially announced. And then, as the tripleheaders take their toll, we face the challenge of keeping countless rosters in our heads and logging the great plays and emotional moments — a task that can be all-consuming.

As the field narrows, trends and heroes emerge, and we can begin to project regional matchups. And before you know it, we're on the road to the Final Four and Super Saturday. After the national semifinals, we regroup and focus on the two survivors and a national prime-time telecast.

Then it's over, all that hoopla and the hollering. A new champion is crowned, and in looking back over the draw, everything seems so logical, even when it's not.

In fact, rarely do the favorites sweep through the field. And that's why we call this American sports pageant "March Madness."

__Jim Nantz__ grew up in Colts Neck, New Jersey, and graduated from the University of Houston with a Communications degree in 1981. In 1982, he was hired by KSL-TV — the CBS affiliate in Salt Lake City — as a sports anchor. In Salt Lake City, he also did play-by-play for Brigham Young University football and Utah Jazz color commentary with Rod Hundley. Nantz was named Utah Sportscaster of the Year in 1985. CBS Sports hired him in 1985. There, he's been host of "The College Football Report" and co-host of the NCAA Basketball Tournament, including the Final Four. He handles commentary for the PGA Tour, as well as play-by-play for the US Open Tennis Championships, the NBA and selected NFL games. Nantz has also done commentary for track and field, swimming and diving, polo and old-timers' baseball games. He is the host for the Cotton and Sun bowls and does NFL games on the CBS Radio Network.

He and his wife, Lorrie, live in Westport, Connecticut.

Seton Hall battles Indiana at the 1989 NCAA West Regionals in Denver's McNichols Sports Arena. Seton Hall was the victor. Photo courtesy of Rich Clarkson/Sports Illustrated.

BLACK AND WHITE AND TECHNICOLOR MEMORIES

Jim Enright, rotund Chicago official, sets down a ruling. Photo from April 1, 1960 **Rocky Mountain News**, *courtesy of The Denver Public Library, Western History Collection.*

IRV BROWN

Working the NCAA Division I basketball tournament was a privilege for me. Indeed, my 22 trips to the tourney and six trips to the Final Four gave me the opportunity to be a part of some great games and to rub shoulders with some outstanding competitors.

Although it's been some time since I've worn my zebra colors, the memories don't seem to fade. In fact, they seem to get more vivid as the years pass. I'd like to share a few of those memories with you.

My first assignment was in Wichita in 1966, where Texas Western beat Oklahoma City University and then went on to beat Kentucky for the national championship. Texas Western's coach, Don Haskins, had a great team that featured five black starting players, which was virtually unheard of in those days.

The level of competition at Wichita in 1966 was high, but it was even better in Lawrence in 1967 when I refed a regional that featured Wes Unseld of Louisville, Jo Jo White of Kansas and "Big E" Elvin Hayes of Houston — players who I knew were "can't miss" NBA players.

I finally advanced out of a regional in 1969 when I got the chance to ref the Marquette-Purdue game in the semifinal. Al McGuire coached the Warriors then, and they appeared to be headed for their first NCAA final before Rick Mount sank a last-second shot in overtime, giving the game to Purdue.

I followed Purdue to the Final Four in Louisville, where the Boilermakers met Dean Smith's North Carolina team. Purdue won and advanced to the final against a UCLA squad led by Lew Alcindor. I worked the final with Mike DeTamasso, who later went on to broadcast New Jersey Nets games, and what I remember most is that it was Alcindor's last college game. He and the Bruins closed on a winning 92-72 note as Lew took home the tournament's MVP award. At the time, I remembered thinking that Alcindor could have played pro ball even if he were only 6′4″ because he handled the basketball so well — he was that talented.

In 1971, I worked the finals at the Astrodome in Houston. My partner was Jim Bain and UCLA beat Villanova for the title.

Three things stand out about these games. First, it was a terrible place to watch a basketball game. Second, Sidney Wicks, Henry Bibby and Curtis Rowe kept talking to each other the whole game, saying things like, "We're not going to be the first team to lose a championship game in UCLA uniforms!" And third, Villanova had to later forfeit its tournament money because its star, Howard Porter, had signed with an agent, which technically made him a professional.

The next year, I worked the regional in Dayton, where Florida State beat Kentucky in what had to be a heartbreaker for a lot of people since it was Wildcats coach Adolph Rupp's last game. I advanced to the Final Four in Los Angeles, where Bobby Scott and I teamed to work the Florida State-UCLA game. The Bruins beat the Seminoles with the help of a big red-

Irv Brown refereed at six NCAA Final Four tournaments and later served as supervisor of officials for the Western Athletic Conference. Left, Brown officiating a North Carolina-Florida State game. Photo courtesy of Rich Clarkson/Sports Illustrated.

headed kid by the name of Bill Walton.

My next assignment came in 1974 when I worked the North Carolina State-Marquette contest. The Wolfpack beat the Warriors in a game that saw some great talent cruise up and down the floor, including David Thompson, Maurice Lucas, Tom Burleson and Monte Towe. I also remember Marquette coach Al McGuire picking up two technical fouls.

In 1976, I worked the All-Big Ten final in Philadelphia featuring Bobby Knight's undefeated Indiana team and archrival Michigan, coached by Bobby Orr. The Hoosiers beat the Wolverines, but not before Bobby Wilkerson got cold-cocked — something my partner Bob Wortman and I never saw. Knight, with his characteristic concern for referees' health and well-being, suggested we eat some carrots.

My last Final Four was in Atlanta in 1977. Marquette won a squeaker from UNC-Charlotte, 51-49, beat University of Nevada-Las Vegas in the semifinal, and went on to win the national title for Al McGuire's swan song from North Carolina, 67-59.

In 1978, I took the supervisor of officials' job with the Western Athletic Conference and accepted no further NCAA assignments after that.

People sometimes ask me if I miss refing. Sure. But every time I watch the finals, I feel good about having been a part of it all at least a few times.

***Irv Brown** has been a fixture on the Denver sports scene for years.*

A North High School graduate who lettered in three sports and won All-City honors in basketball, he attended Garden City Junior College and the University of Northern Colorado.

Brown coached Denver-area high school and college football, basketball and baseball teams for several years, and later made his mark as a basketball official, working six NCAA Final Four tournaments and serving as supervisor of officials for the Western Athletic Conference.

He has spent the last few years as a broadcaster, acting as sports director at several Denver radio stations, and doing commentary for ESPN, CBS, the Prime Sports Network, Raycom, the Continental Basketball Association and the Denver Nuggets.

He also hosts a daily sports-talk show on KYBG in Denver.

INDIANA AND KENTUCKY BASKETBALL PLAYERS

JIM BURRIS

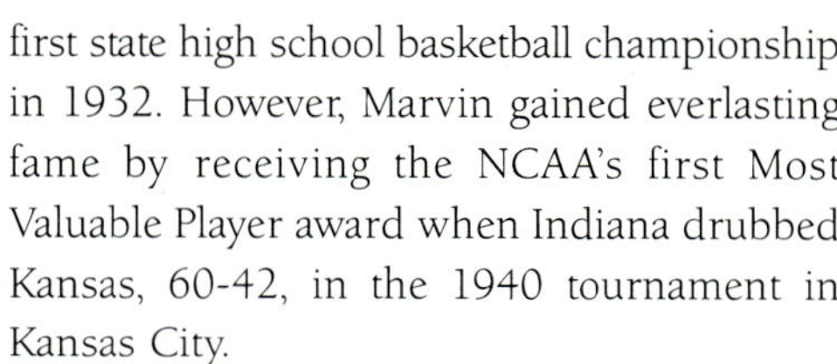

*Opposite: Indiana coach Bobby Knight has a characteristic conversation with the referee. Photo courtesy of Rich Clarkson/***Sports Illustrated***.*

While I've pretty much made a living through baseball, football and some professional golf, my first love has always been college basketball, particularly as it's played in Indiana and Kentucky where I lived before moving to Colorado in the late 1950s.

On learning that Denver had been awarded a 1989 NCAA regional, as well as the 1990 Final Four tournament, a flood of basketball memories rushed to mind and so, when tourney chairman Roger Kinney asked me to write a piece for *Rocky Mountain Basketball*, I was quick to say yes.

I lived and attended high school in one of the basketball-mad towns in the Midwest — New Castle, Indiana. This hamlet of barely 20,000 spawned five All-Americans, including Kent Benson and Steve Alford, who paced Indiana University to NCAA crowns in 1976 and 1987, respectively. Indeed, the state of Indiana's basketball Hall of Fame recently was moved from Indianapolis to New Castle thanks to Benson's and Alford's achievements, and because it's the birthplace of one of the sport's most renowned families, the Huffmans. Two of the Huffmans, Vernon and Marvin, took their talents to Indiana University, where they were consensus All-Americans. The youngest, Gilbert, tired of following in his famous brothers' footsteps, went to Tennessee, where he, too, won All-American honors.

Vernon, who also was an All-American halfback at Bloomington, led New Castle to its first state high school basketball championship in 1932. However, Marvin gained everlasting fame by receiving the NCAA's first Most Valuable Player award when Indiana drubbed Kansas, 60-42, in the 1940 tournament in Kansas City.

That tourney also was the first to make money, inasmuch as the 1939 event — held on Northwestern University's campus and won by Oregon — lost about $2,500. The 1940 teams split a profit of $9,490, and the Big Show was on its way. Since then, it has always made money, and today, Final Four tickets may be the toughest to obtain in all of collegiate and professional sports.

Some 13 seasons passed before Indiana took another title. Again, Kansas was victimized, this time by a 69-68 margin in Kansas City. The win gave coach Branch McCracken his second championship trophy and generated a lot of ink for his stars, Don Schlundt and Bobby Leonard.

The late 1940s belonged to the man who always wore a brown suit — Adolph Rupp, who built a basketball dynasty in Lexington, Kentucky. Along with a jillion Southeastern Conference titles, the Baron won four NCAA championships and stacked up more wins than any coach before or since.

Of all his great teams, Rupp contended to his dying day in 1977 that his "Fabulous Five" of the 1948-49 season was "the greatest college team of all time." Rupp's contention is clearly open to debate, but it's a fact that his magnificent starting five of Alex Groza, Wah Wah Jones, Ralph Beard, Cliff Barker and Ken Rollins not only took back-to-back NCAA titles, but carried most of the load in the United States' victorious march through the 1948 Olympics. Furthermore, the Kentuckians then marched into professional basketball as a unit and won a championship under the banner of the Indianapolis Olympians.

In one stretch, Rupp's teams compiled an amazing 125-12 won-lost record. (Only John Wooden had more success in NCAA competition.) And no doubt, Adolph surely had more All-Americans than any other coach. Along with Beard, Groza and Jones, his other standouts were Vern Hatton, Johnny Cox, Bill Spivey, Cliff Hagan, Frank Ramsey, Lou Dampier and the present coach of the Los Angeles Lakers, Pat Riley.

Always a contender, Kentucky won a fifth championship in 1978, downing Duke, 94-88, under Joe B. Hall, who had once coached at Denver's Regis College.

Indiana — paced by Kent Benson and Scott May, who combined for 51 points — defeated Michigan, 86-68, in the 1976 finals in Philadelphia. It was the first of Coach Bobby Knight's three national championships to date and marked one of the few times any winner has come through a season unscathed. For the year, the Hoosiers went 32-0 after being ranked No. 1 in pre-season polls.

At the end of that storybook year, Indiana's fine guard, Quinn Buckner, exulted, "After all this, if we don't deserve the national championship, I don't know who does. You can't do more than win 'em all."

Knight won his second title in Philly's Spectrum in 1981. Helping Indiana defeat a good North Carolina team, 63-60, were Landon Turner and Isiah Thomas, who now puts his considerable talents to work for the Detroit Pistons.

Indiana won its fifth NCAA crown in 1987 by nipping a courageous Syracuse squad, 74-73, in the New Orleans Superdome. Keith Smart scored the winning basket at the buzzer, but Steve Alford drew most of the praise after starting for four years and becoming the school's all-time leading scorer with 2,438 points. Only two people in the state of Indiana's major college basketball history scored more — Larry Bird, who had 2,850 career points at Indiana State, and Austin Carr of Notre Dame, who tallied 2,560. Incidentally, Bird, the pride of French Lick, and his 1979 Indiana State team made it to the NCAA title game before bowing to Michigan State and Earvin "Magic" Johnson, 75-64.

Coach Adolph Rupp (fifth from left) of Kentucky and some of his "runts" looking dejected as the 1966 championship slips away to Texas Western, 72-65. Lexington Herald-Leader *photo, reproduced from* They Were No. 1 *by Robert Stern.*

No recap of Indiana-Kentucky basketball triumphs would be fair or complete without some reference to the Louisville team and its quality coach, Denny Crum, who have won a pair of championships. The Cardinals' biggest victory came in 1980 when they handed UCLA a rare tournament defeat in the finale, 59-54. Then, Crum and Co. took title No. 2 in 1986 by downing Duke, 72-69.

So, all in all, during the 50-year history of the competition, Indiana and Kentucky schools have collected a dozen NCAA titles. However, Kentucky's Wildcats are collegiate basketball's all-time leader in victories with 1,453, and their winning percentage of .761 is also the nation's best.

Ironically, the man who stood tallest in NCAA tournament action was a Hoosier by birth — UCLA coaching legend John Wooden. From 1964 to 1975, his Bruins captured 10 titles. Among the luminaries he sent to the pro ranks were Lew Alcindor — who later became Kareem Abdul-Jabbar — Bill Walton, Gail Goodrich and Walt Hazzard.

Before migrating to California, Wooden had coached high school ball in Indiana, and in the late 1940s, twice guided Indiana State to the

*Kentucky and St. Johns mix it up at the 1985 NCAA West Regional Tournament at Denver's McNichols Sports Arena. Photo courtesy of Rich Clarkson/*Sports Illustrated.

NAIA small college finals, where one of his losses was administered by Larry Varnell's Regis College team.

When Kansas, a frequent Final Four participant, finally took it all in 1952, the star was an Indianan, Clyde Lovellette — the only national scoring champion ever to play on a championship team.

For me, the 1959 tournament in Louisville was especially memorable since it featured All-Americans Jerry West of West Virginia and Oscar Robertson of Cincinnati. Both were magnificent in losing efforts as California took the championship, nipping the West Virginia Mountaineers, 71-70, in the final game.

As in life and in all sports, luck and circumstance play big roles, and I know that hundreds of brilliant basketballers haven't been fortunate enough to play on teams that reached the college finals — a list that includes Hank Luisetti of Stanford, Ed Macauley of St. Louis, Vince Boryla of Notre Dame and Denver, Dick Groat of Duke, Walter Dukes of Seton Hall, Sihugo Green of Duquesne, Walt Bellamy of Indiana, Rick Barry of Miami, Spencer Haywood of Detroit, Pete Maravich of LSU, and the incomparable Julius Erving of Massachusetts.

But the fact that they played the game — and in many cases, elevated it thanks to their individual talents — helped make basketball the sweet poetry it is. And for that, we can all be thankful.

***Jim Burris** was born in New Castle, Indiana in 1922 and attended Kansas Junior College, the University of Georgia and the University of Missouri, where he majored in journalism.*

He has been a baseball reporter for The Sporting News, *the president of baseball's American Association, a special assistant to former baseball commissioner Ford Frick, and president of the Texas League.*

From 1965 through 1984, Burris was general manager of the legendary Denver Bears baseball club, which, among its many accomplishments, led all minor league teams in attendance in 1981 and drew an all-time single-game record 65,666 fans on July 3, 1982.

The Sporting News *named Burris its Minor League Executive of the Year in 1980, and he was named the American Association's top executive four times.*

A Denver resident, Burris is now a sports columnist with The Denver Business Journal.

PROFILE OF OSCAR ROBERTSON

JAMES B. MEADOW

Oscar Robertson was an All-American and the College Player of the Year for all three of his varsity seasons at the University of Cincinnati. His pro career included 10 seasons with the Cincinnati Royals and 4 seasons with the Milwaukee Bucks.

Greatness knows itself
— *William Shakespeare*

Shakespeare had it right — greatness *does* know itself. But there are degrees of greatness; sometimes it's so enormous, so prodigious, it allows even ordinary mortals to instantly know it.

Such was the case with Oscar Palmer Robertson, a basketball player whose greatness was so relentlessly incandescent, so utterly galvanizing, that anyone who saw him in action could bear immediate witness to it. From the heartland to the hinterland, from the Big Apple to Big Sur — and back and forth between them — Robertson's eloquence on the court made him the poet laureate of the game.

Remember those enormous, doe-like eyes that saw everything? The quicksilver moves? The fluid grace? The passes that moved as if guided by radar? The flawless shots that singed the nets? And what about those sharp and none-too-reluctant elbows to provide the perfect counterpoint to his on-court symphony? Granted, it's the conceit of every generation of sports fans to lay claim to having grown up with the Greatest Player of All Time. But face it — those of us who want to make a case for Oscar Robertson are on rock-solid ground.

Take Magic Johnson and mix him with Michael Jordan and you have an idea of what kind of player the Big O was. Want a resume and statistics? He was an All-American and the College Player of the Year for all three of his varsity seasons at the University of Cincinnati. (Remember back in the dark ages when freshmen were ineligible?)

During that collegiate career, he led the nation in scoring every year. For the record, he averaged more than 30 points, 15 rebounds and seven assists each game. In 1960, he co-captained and led the US Olympic basketball team — which many say was the best ever — to an easy gold medal.

Then he turned pro and, typically, didn't miss a beat. En route to being named NBA Rookie of the Year with the Cincinnati Royals, he established a first-year assist record that stood 27 seasons. He was NBA MVP for 1963-64, played in 12 All-Star games (in which he was three times named MVP) and, after 14 luminous seasons, retired with per-game averages of 25.7 points, 7.5 rebounds and 9.5 assists.

But as convenient as they are for filling up the sports archives and settling the odd wager in a tavern, statistics are a sterile refuge when you're talking about a player like Oscar Robertson. Sure, the numbers count for something, but you have to put them into perspective and take into account the context in which they were achieved. Consider, for example, his first trip to Madison Square Garden. There he was, a college sophomore playing in the Parthenon of Hoops in front of a seething crowd of self-appointed basketball experts. The perfect spot for a case of the jitters, for the Big O to become the Big Zero, right?

Not exactly.

True, Robertson wasn't perfect — he did miss a few shots. Not that anybody was counting the misses. You see, in his New York debut, all Oscar did was connect for a Garden record of 56 points. Sophomore jitters, indeed.

The virtuosity of Robertson's game was complemented by his utter aplomb. Before Oscar's senior year in college, Dr. Kenneth Wilson, dean of Cincinnati's college of business administration, observed, "People like Oscar have a great driving desire to be a champion. Some would call it aggressiveness. I'd rather think of it as maturity and poise. He's had to develop remarkable maturity to withstand the assaults of his publicity."

Not that this "remarkable maturity" was always in evidence on the court. Robertson's reputation as a whiner and complainer are a well-documented part of basketball lore, and didn't exactly endear him to referees. According to an article in *The Saturday Evening Post*, "He is always griping at the referees. After a bad call, he goes through a startling transformation right on court. The incomparable graceful athlete becomes an ungainly sorehead. . . . " Of course, when you play basketball in the rarified realms that Robertson did, winning is the bottom line, not good conduct. As Adolph Rupp once growled, "You get no points for sportsmanship."

But to dwell on Robertson's histrionics would be a gross injustice. It was only part of his court persona — and a lesser part at that. Most of the time, he was an amalgam of grace and skill. In fact, because he was so regal out there, any deviation from his silken style called immediate and disproportionate attention to itself.

Take for example, his toughness.

To clean up a playground parlance, Oscar took no guff out there. Mess with him and he'd mess right back. There was none of that turning-the-other-cheek business with the Big O. Some might even have said that Robertson had a mean streak. Maybe so. But more to the point, what he also had was the fire in the belly, a sizzling competitive drive. Most times, his consummate skills rendered the rough stuff unnecessary — Oscar could beat anyone because he was flat out so much better than everyone. But woe unto the hit men who persisted. A rock-hard 6'5" Robertson was perfectly capable of mixing it up. In fact, his size — unusual for a backcourt man of the times — made him the prototype of today's "big guard."

But even if Robertson was bigger than most of the guards of his day, size alone wasn't what fueled his excellence. He had an almost preternatural feel for the game; his devotion to basketball made him seem like some sort of mystic. As a young man, he even avoided movies for the sake of his eyes, and he rarely touched alcohol lest his precision reflexes be tainted. His practice regimen was just this side of fanatical. For Robertson, hoops was no game; it was a calling.

Oscar Robertson, playing for the University All-Stars, goes up for a jump shot at the 1960 Olympic tryouts against the Phillips 66ers. Photo by Mel Schieltz, April 1, 1960 Rocky Mountain News, *courtesy of the Denver Public Library, Western History Collection.*

One story about the young O had him watching in horror as a friend dribbled a leather basketball on an outdoor court. Oscar grabbed the ball away and admonished the friend because the hard surface could "ruin the feel of the ball." Perhaps this story is apocryphal; a player of Robertson's stature often generates a host of exaggerated anecdotes. But given Robertson's passionate love affair with basketball, perhaps the story isn't.

Ultimately, Robertson's reverence for the "feel" of a basketball was less important than the magic he could perform with it. And, as is so often the case with the immortals, the grander the stage, the more dazzling was Oscar's performance. Witness the 1960 Olympic Basketball Trials.

Convened in Denver, the trials attracted the crème de la crème of amateur basketball. The likes of Jerry West, Jerry Lucas, John Havlicek, Walt Bellamy, Terry Dischinger, Adrian Smith and Zelmo Beatty were among the cast of 96 Olympic hopefuls. Amid this kind of all-star gathering you'd figure it would be hard for one name to dominate the marquee. Unless, that is, the name was Oscar Robertson. As one local columnist put it, the hordes that attended the games were drawn in part by the desire to see "if Oscar is as good as his press clippings."

He was.

Seizing center stage, Robertson gave a series of bravura performances. Shooting? Passing? Rebounding? He did it all. Against the best his country had to offer, the Big O gave clinic after clinic. And, just like the Madison Square

Opposite: An elated Oscar Robertson after controlling the 1955 Indiana title game where Crispus Attucks was the first black high school to win the state championship. Photo by Frank H. Fisse. Reproduced with permission from Hoosiers, The Fabulous Basketball Life of Indiana *by Phillip M. Hoose.*

Garden skeptics years earlier, whatever doubters there were in Denver came away converted to true believers, their jaws dropping lower in amazement with each game. Of course, once the Rome Olympics began, that amazement became worldwide. Led by Robertson, the US team spindled, folded and mutilated the opposition and struck gold in a big way.

The trip to the winner's podium at the Olympics was Robertson's first championship stroll since he had led Indianapolis' Crispus Attucks High School to consecutive state titles. Much to his chagrin — and to the glee of Robertson detractors — the Big O never came away with college basketball's brass ring. Oh, he had come close. As a sophomore, Cincinnati was eliminated in a second-round overtime game against Kansas State. And the following year, the Bearcats clawed their way to the Final Four before California eliminated them.

Yet, the four-year championship hiatus between high school and the Olympics would be dwarfed by the drought of Robertson's professional career. In his 14 seasons — ten with the Cincinnati Royals, four with the Milwaukee Bucks — Oscar Robertson, arguably the greatest player to ever play the game of basketball, won just one title. But then, that lone championship — coming as it did in the 1970-71 season, late in his career — may have been all the sweeter for its exclusivity.

The matter of championships aside, Robertson's professional tenure was one more endorsement of his basketball talent, the last step on that progression of greatness. Still, if the road over which he maneuvered his way toward expanding excellence was a continuous one, it was not free from the bumps of poverty or the hairpin turns of social injustice.

The youngest of three boys, Oscar was born near Charlotte, Tennessee. When he was four, the family moved to the northwest ghetto of Indianapolis, where his father got a job working for the city sanitation department. Oscar's first foray into basketball came when he was six and his brother Bailey put up a peach basket on the back of the family's tar paper-roofed house. Money was far from plentiful for the Robertsons, meaning toys were often a product of imagination and ingenuity.

The first Robertson "basketball" was actually made of rags secured by elastic, although, as Bailey would remember years later, sometimes "we'd get real lucky and find an old broken tennis ball in some alley."

His mother was only too glad that Oscar and his brothers latched on to the game. Their economically depressed neighborhood was rife with far too many temptations. Once the boys were old enough, Mazell Robertson saw to it that they had membership cards at the Senate Avenue YMCA. When they weren't at the Y, the kids were usually down at the "Dust Bowl," a vacant lot where local pick-up games were the crucible in which players could prove themselves.

When Oscar was 11, his parents divorced. His mother, a licensed beautician by trade, took on a part-time job cooking for a white family. One magical evening, she came home with a present for her sons: a basketball that one of her employer's children had grown disenchanted with. For Oscar, that night was a watershed. Some boys have puppies to befriend; Oscar Robertson had his ball.

"He was always bouncing it," Mazell Robertson recalled. "He'd bring it to the dinner table, and he took it to bed with him. When the sound of the bumping stopped, we knew that Oscar was ready to go to sleep."

By the time Oscar reached Crispus Attucks High, it was lights out for the competition. He led the team to 45 straight victories and two Indiana titles. The championships won by Crispus Attucks were the first ever by an all-black school. (For the record, it's both ironic and appropriate that Crispus Attucks High blazed a trail of sorts by winning those titles. Its namesake, a former slave, was the first of five people slain during the Boston Massacre of 1770. Consequently, some historians consider Attucks to be the first man to sacrifice his life for the cause of American freedom.)

Oscar Robertson with Denver Manual High School coach Rudy Carey at the 1988 Mile High Classic. Photo courtesy of Fritz Law.

Robertson's prep career closed with his being named "Mr. Basketball" in Indiana — a title the Hoosier state holds in great esteem — as well as the "Star of Stars" in the annual Indiana-Kentucky all-star competition.

As he navigated his way toward maturity as a man and as a basketball player, Robertson became someone inclined to keep his own counsel. His mother once remarked, "There's a lot going on inside Oscar that I don't know. There's a lot I do know, but only because I'm his mother, not because he tells me." To this, his brother Henry added, "Oz is a sort of a reticent person. He lives a lot inside himself. He doesn't trust too many people. There are things inside Oscar he doesn't discuss, even with his own family."

Today Robertson is active in community affairs and heads several businesses. Photo courtesy of Fritz Law.

Robertson's reserve could be unsettling to some; there were those who found him aloof, glum, sullen. In 1959, during Robertson's senior year in college, when he had scarcely turned 21, one national magazine saw fit to run a profile of him under the title "Basketball's Moody Marvel."

Part of Robertson's "moodiness" stemmed, no doubt, from his keen awareness of racism. Though he was the University of Cincinnati's star player, he was made to feel unwelcome in various campus hangouts. Even more insulting, once he had to endure the indignity of segregated accommodations when the team played in Houston. Following that experience, Robertson made it clear that the next time something like that happened, he'd be long gone from the team.

It was typical of Robertson that his response to this instance, and others of racial injustice was unfailingly direct. If he wasn't quite militant, he certainly wasn't the passive victim. As the boy gave way to the man, Robertson's insistence upon getting his due measure of respect was an essential ingredient of his dignity. The player who took no guff on the court would take none off it, either. He was a proud man, unafraid to show that pride.

Robertson's refusal to back down extended to his dealings with the Cincinnati Royals' front office. During one protracted contract tiff, Robertson let it be known that he was prepared to sit out the season, a radical threat in those days, but one which few doubted he was capable of fulfilling. What made his resolve all the more impressive was, as one person close to him observed at that time, "Given Oscar's tax situation, the amount [of money] involved wasn't really that important. It was primarily a matter of principle." Although the dispute was resolved in time for Oscar to play the season, the settlement didn't represent acquiescence on Robertson's part; his principles were not compromised. (Undoubtedly this unwavering fidelity to his beliefs was what led to Robertson's election — and 10-year reign — as president of the NBA Players Association.)

The toughness and integrity and intelligence that stamped Robertson as a player and negotiator have followed him since his departure from the sport. In fact, maybe the best part of the Oscar Robertson Saga is its life-after-basketball postscript. Unlike some athletes who wind up adrift after their glory days have passed them by, Robertson found new worlds to conquer as a businessman.

Currently, he is president of no less than three successful companies — a general contracting firm, a trucking company and an industrial chemical cleaning supplies manufacturer and distributor. He is also on the board of directors of an investment company money fund with assets in excess of $300 million. Coupled with these corporate achievements are his myriad community-service associations that have ranged from the Red Cross to the Boy Scouts to the NAACP to the American Cancer Society. To these impressive accomplishments can be added the avalanche of basketball citations that have been heaped upon him since his retirement. He belongs to the High School, Olympic and NBA halls of fame. He's been named to the All-Time Madison Square Garden Team. And he's on the NCAA All-Time All-Star Team.

But this is all yesterday's news, and men like Oscar Robertson are usually found looking ahead toward tomorrow. Right now, at 51, the hair is grayer, but the eyes are still large and all-seeing, and the appetite for success is as prodigious as ever. In short, Oscar Robertson is still on the move, destined for big things.

How big?

Who can say?

Well, one man can.

Chances are, Oscar Robertson has a pretty good idea of what lies ahead for him. Remember, as Shakespeare said, greatness knows itself.

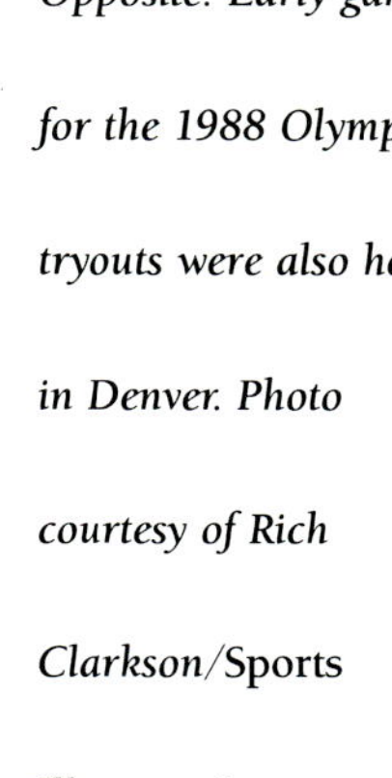

***Opposite:** Early games for the 1988 Olympic tryouts were also held in Denver. Photo courtesy of Rich* **Clarkson/Sports Illustrated.**

A native New Yorker and graduate of Brooklyn College and Columbia University's Graduate School of Journalism, ***James B. Meadow*** *was a short, slow playmaker back in those pre-historic times when there was no such thing as a "point" guard. Today, he is a Denver-based writer who is currently at work on a novel and a book about sports team owners.*

USA
BASKETBALL

OLYMPIC TRYOUTS, THE BEST EVER

JOHN RAYBURN

Players view the Olympic flag before the beginning of the 1960 Olympic tryouts held in Denver. Photo from the March 31, 1960 Rocky Mountain News, *courtesy of Denver Public Library, Western History Collection.*

The 1960 Olympic basketball trials were held at the Denver Coliseum in late March and early April, and I had the good fortune to broadcast the games with the late John Henry on KOA Radio.

A total of eight teams of 12 players — 96 candidates for the dozen Olympic spots — gathered for the shootout. They included the Peoria Cats — sponsored by the Caterpillar Tractor Co. — of the National Industrial Basketball League, who had just won the AAU championship by defeating the NIBL's Akron Goodyears, 115-93. Another league powerhouse, Phillips 66, joined the elite group, along with the NCAA champion Ohio State Buckeyes, the NCAA University All-Stars, the NAIA All-Stars and the Armed Forces All-Stars.

That stellar cast of university stars was headed by Oscar Robertson of Cincinnati and Jerry West of West Virginia; 6'11" centers Darrall Imhoff of California and Walt Bellamy of Indiana; Big Ten scoring champion Terry Dischinger of Purdue; powerful Tom "Satch" Sanders of NYU; St. John's All-American Tony Jackson; forwards Ron Johnson of Minnesota and Tom Stith of St. Bonaventure; and guards Jay Arnett of Texas, Jim Darrow of Bowling Green and Roger Kaiser of Georgia Tech.

Of course, the other teams were loaded, too. The three NIBL clubs had stockpiled the leading AAU talent and they also were allowed to beef up their rosters by adding top players from other teams. For example, Les Lane of Wichita Vickers was selected by Phillips, which also had University of Colorado great Burdie Haldorson on its list of regulars. Lane eventually played with and coached the Denver-Chicago Truckers AAU team.

Ohio State — which had just beaten California for the NCAA crown — was led by Jerry Lucas, John Havlicek and Larry Siegfried. Wayne Hightower of Kansas was a stalwart for the NCAA All-Stars, and Zelmo Beatty of Prairie View and Porter Merriweather of Tennessee A&I were the NAIA's standouts.

The NAIA squad came through with a startling upset of Ohio State's classy college champs in the opening round, 76-69, using a tight zone defense that sagged on All-American sophomore center Lucas, holding him to 13 points. Part of the blame for the Buckeyes' loss was pinned on coach Fred Taylor, who showed little concern before the game. It turned out that he had taken a trip to Colorado Springs that morning to play golf at the Broadmoor, a round that lasted only seven holes thanks to a snowstorm.

In other first-round action, Akron, tired from the AAU tournament, struggled to get by the Armed Forces, 82-76, even though guard Adrian Smith of the service team scored a game-high 21 points.

Next came the game everyone had been waiting for — the clash between the University All-Stars and always-tough Phillips. Nearly 10,000 fans, who paid from $1 to $3 for tickets, turned out because, as the late Jim Graham wrote in *The Denver Post*, they

John Prudhoe (12) of the Peoria Cats grabs a rebound against the NAIA All-Stars' Rudy Davalon as the Cats went on to win this round of the 1960 Olympic tryouts, 89-68. Photo by Dick Davis, April 2, 1960 Rocky Mountain News, *courtesy of Denver Public Library, Western History Collection.*

Coach Alex Hannum pleads with his team to take charge in their game with the University All-Stars. Photo by Dick Davis, April 2, 1960 Rocky Mountain News, *courtesy of Denver Public Library, Western History Collection.*

wanted to see for themselves "if Oscar is as good as his press clippings."

It turned out that the Big O was even better as he and his mates crushed the proud 66ers, 96-79. Robertson — who had rewritten the collegiate scoring book in his three years at Cincy — tallied only 23 against Phillips, but he took an 11-minute rest in the second half after he showed off his skills as a passer, shot blocker, defender and rebounder.

The seven-hour, four-game session ended as the Peoria Cats struggled past the NCAA All-Stars, 91-89. The Cats were outscored by 10 baskets from the field, but dropped in 37 of 44 free throw attempts to nail down the win. Indeed, Peoria's Bob Boozer made 17 of 18 from the line, including 13 in a row in the second half.

The next day, Phillips, coached by Bud Browning, regained a measure of respect by stopping the Armed Forces, 88-74, as on-loan guard Lane provided floor leadership and Haldorson notched 17 points. Ohio State also bounced back by tripping up the NCAA All-Stars, 89-79, as all five Buckeye starters scored in double figures — Havlicek led the way with 24 — and Lucas grabbed 22 rebounds.

In the evening's third game, the University Stars tromped, 103-88, over Akron. Robertson had 29 points and West 22 and the Stars outrebounded the Goodyears, 67-42. After the game Alex Hannum, the coach of Wichita

Youngsters eagerly collect autographs from Tony Jackson of St. John's of Brooklyn and Oscar Robertson of Cincinnati University at the Olympic tryouts. Photo by Dick Davis, April 2, 1960 Rocky Mountain News, *courtesy of Denver Public Library, Western History Collection.*

In the game for fifth place in the 1960 Olympic trials, the ball is loose as players from Ohio State and the AAU Phillips 66ers vie for possession. The Buckeyes won, 87-77. Photo by Dick Davis, April 3, 1960 Rocky Mountain News, *courtesy of Denver Public Library, Western History Collection.*

Vickers, said, "Walt Bellamy looks about as fine a big man as has come along in some time. I would compare him with Bill Russell and Wilt Chamberlain." All that the 6'11" Hoosier ace had done up to that point was score 35 points and pull down 25 rebounds in the trials.

The Peoria Cats won their semifinal game, demolishing the NAIA team, 89-68.

A lot would be riding on the next game with Robertson and Co. Cats coach Warren Womble was confident his men would win.

The next night, seventh place in the trials went to the Armed Forces as they ran past the NCAA All-Stars, 98-85, with Adrian Smith contributing 25 points. Fifth place went to Ohio State after the Buckeyes humiliated Phillips, 87-77, and Akron's easy 88-77 win over the NAIA Stars nailed down third place.

Heading into the title game, the University All-Stars had been labeled the greatest college team ever assembled, and they proved everyone right, annihilating Peoria, 124-97. The Big O had 20 points, and Jerry West pumped in 15 of 21 shots from the floor and nine of 12 free throw attempts for a game-high 39 points.

Winning coach Pete Newell was elated. After leading his California Bears to the NCAA title the year before and to second place in the 1960 NCAA tournament, he had given up college coaching to take over as Cal's athletic director. He had initially declined the offer to coach the University Stars but later gave in. After winning the Olympic trials title he grinned and told the press, "I'm glad I reconsidered."

From the playoffs Newell wound up with a 12-man squad of Robertson, Dischinger, Imhoff, West, J.R. Nette of Texas, Bellamy, Lucas, Boozer, Haldorson, Allen Kelley of the University of Kansas and the Armed Services All-Stars, Lane and Smith.

At the Olympics in Rome, Newell's men marched past Italy, Japan, Hungary, Yugoslavia and Uruguay before the showdown with the Russians. The United States' smallest margin of victory before the big meeting had been 34 points, and the Americans once led Yugoslavia 32-3. Indeed, Robertson, West and Lucas sat down shortly after the start of the second half in most games.

The USSR was almost as easy, as Newell's men won, 81-57. As one Soviet player said later, "We run when we get the ball. The Americans run before they get it." An anticlimactic victory over Brazil sewed up the gold medal, and Newell said, "It wasn't the coaching. I just pointed these guys [in the right direction] and let 'em go."

Each team member wound up in the US Olympic Hall of Fame, and just five years later, seven of them played in the NBA All-Star game.

The best ever? Who can argue?

***John Rayburn** could be labeled "Mr. Versatility." With more than 42 years broadcasting experience, he is the only person to anchor the 10 PM news on all three of Denver's network affiliates.*

He also has done play-by-play broadcasts of Colorado State University, Air Force Academy and University of Wyoming football, pre-season TV games of the Denver Broncos, University of Denver hockey, Denver Bears baseball, and the US Open and PGA golf tournaments. He also broadcast the 1960 US Olympic basketball trials. He is now a spokesman for several major companies and has made countless speaking appearances for leading firms and organizations across the country.

DENVER - 1840
HOW THE WEST WAS REALLY WON...
KADUNK
THERE. H-O-R-S-E. HA! YOU LOSE!
SAL
drew litton
ROCKY MOUNTAIN NEWS

COLORADO HIGH SCHOOL BASKETBALL

BERT BORGMANN

It might seem inconceivable that for at least one day, the focus of a nation's basketball fans could be on a tiny town in northern Colorado. But it happened in 1924, and the town was Windsor, an agricultural hamlet northwest of Greeley.

The Bulldogs — or as they would become known during that season, the Wizards — captured the national high school championship in Chicago, whipping Yankton, South Dakota, 25-6.

Before they returned to Windsor, the Wizards were treated to a five-mile long procession featuring 5,000 fans, 100 automobiles, two bands and a huge celebration in front of the Greeley courthouse.

Perhaps it was at this juncture that Colorado high school basketball came to the fore. Perhaps it began the year before when Windsor won two games in the national tournament before bowing out. Or perhaps it began in the late 1890s when Dr. James Naismith, who invented the game, accepted a position directing the Denver YMCA's athletic program. Whenever it began, Colorado and high school basketball have enjoyed a love affair spanning the generations.

The Wizards of Windsor became the first team from the West to win the title on that wonderful night of April 5, 1924. One wire report of the game called the 25-6 victory "the most impressive defensive game ever displayed by a national tournament winner." Indeed, after giving up a basket in the first two minutes of the first quarter, the Wizards shut down Yankton until the third minute of the fourth quarter.

The national championship capped two extraordinary seasons which also included two state championships — the only Colorado titles WHS would ever win. For coach Joe Ryan, the win was especially sweet. Soon after the game ended, reporters informed him that his wife had given birth to a daughter.

Colorado basketball again appeared on the national scene in 1926, when state champion Pueblo Central High School finished second in the national championships. Its star player, the legendary Earl "Dutch" Clark, scored more than half his team's points on several occasions, and today, many still consider him the greatest athlete to ever come from a Colorado high school.

In 1929, another team from Colorado's eastern plains captivated hoop fans across the country when Joes — just east of Cope and a few miles northwest of Kirk in Yuma County — captured the state title, and finished third in the national tournament.

Joes won the Colorado state title again in 1930, but a ruling by the young Colorado High School Activities Association kept the team from making another trip to the nationals.

Joes' devotion to basketball ran deep. The school had no gymnasium. The practice court was dirt, and the only time the team missed practice was during a blizzard. Joes was coached by Lane Sullivan, a young man who

Pueblo Central High School's star player in 1926, Earl "Dutch" Clark, led his basketball team to the state championship and to a second place finish in the national tournament. Today, many still consider him the greatest athlete to ever come from a Colorado high school. Photo by William Kuenzel, Detroit News, *courtesy of Pro Football Hall of Fame and Bert Borgmann.*

"JOES HIGH SCHOOL IS HAILED AS WONDER TEAM" read the headline on the March 18, 1929 Denver Post *reporting on the team with no gym that captured the state title and finished third in the national tournament. Photo courtesy of Albert G. Hill.*

literally coached out of a book written by Forrest "Phog" Allen which the Kansas coach had sent in response to a letter from Sullivan.

To overcome the strange bounces a dirt court can give a basketball, the team developed an exemplary passing game. Indeed, the boys from Joes would practice plays until they could run them in their sleep, and Sullivan would officiate scrimmages so closely that his players seldom fouled.

Colorado created its state basketball title in 1918 after Boulder Prep High School had soundly beaten all of its local opponents and went looking for more competition. Boosters from the University of Colorado rounded up ten teams from across the state for a round-robin tournament in which Colorado Springs beat Boulder in the championship game. Colorado Springs also won the next two titles, and Greeley took the crown in 1921.

The success of this new state tournament concept prompted the creation of the Colorado High School Activities Association (which became the Colorado High School Athletic Conference in 1943) and with it, the birth of one of the state's most popular and enduring sporting events.

It was prophetic, perhaps, that Greeley won the first sanctioned championship in 1922, the first of eight for the Wildcats. Counting the 1921 state title, Greeley, which is now Greeley Central, has won nine state championships; only Denver's Manual High School (formerly Manual Training High School) has won as many.

The state's schools played the first 20 championships in a single classification until 1938 when Colorado divided schools into "A" and "B" groups, the latter comprising smaller institutions. Denver North won the first "A" title with a last-second win over Longmont, while Englewood was the first "B" champion. Since then, the state has separated its schools into as many as five divisions, and will have six beginning in 1991.

Perhaps the most exciting game played in state competition came in 1943 when Denver East won its first title with a 30-28 win over Denver North in triple overtime. The two teams were tied at 28-28 after the second OT, so it was mutually agreed that the first team to score in the third extra period would win. Ed Sheehy promptly sank a pair of free throws and East was crowned king.

One of the greatest comebacks in tournament history came in 1954 when heavily favored Englewood was leading Ft. Collins by 20 points midway through the third period. The Lambkins then cut the lead to 16 by the end of that stanza, surged ahead with 23 seconds left in the game on a jumper by Bill Rhoten, and downed the Pirates, 59-57.

All too often, the state's larger schools have received more attention at tournament time than their smaller rivals. But those smaller schools have provided quite a bit of excitement over the years.

Defending "A" champion Brush entered the 1963 finals riding a 41-game winning streak. But archrival, Yuma, which had fallen victim to the Beetdiggers several times in regular season play, turned back Brush, 57-54, to win its second state title in five years.

Branson, a school with just 32 students and only five basketball players, captivated the state in 1967 with a 59-57 overtime win over Walsh. In a classic struggle, no more than four points ever separated the teams throughout the contest. With the score tied 55-55 after regulation, Branson jumped out to a 58-55 lead and began to stall. A free throw with less than two minutes left gave the Bearcats a four-point lead, but Walsh scored a basket with 35 seconds and seemed to have momemtum remaining. Branson, however, was able to run out the clock and win its only state title.

Several schools have established strong basketball traditions, but none stronger than Denver Manual and Greeley Central. Manual has nine state titles to its credit in 18 cham-

Denver's Manual High School 1987-88 "AAAA" State Champion team. Photo by Zemi Photographics, courtesy of Grant Wittenwyler.

pionship game appearances, while the Wildcats have won nine of their 13 title games. It's interesting to note that Jim Baggot took Greeley Central to 14 consecutive state tournaments from 1949 to 1962, winning five times.

In all, six schools have won five or more state championships in more than 70 years of tournament play. Tiny Merino has seven; so does Denver South. Denver East and Denver Christian each have five championships.

For more than two decades, it was easy to identify two regions in the state that dominated play. From 1941 to 1963, no team outside the Denver Prep or Northern leagues won a championship in the state's largest classification. Wheat Ridge, which broke the stranglehold in 1963, was the first suburban school to win a title in the state's largest classification. Since then, more than half of the largest classification championships have been won by other suburban Denver or Colorado Springs schools.

Colorado high school basketball moved in a new direction in 1976 when the state sanctioned girls basketball. The first champions were Golden, "AAA"; Wray, "AA"; and Camp, "A."

Wray High School was certainly the most dominating team of the first five years of girls basketball competition, winning the first four "AA" championships. The Eagles, experts at executing coach Charlotte Jergensen's offense-breaking press, are the only girls team to win more than three state titles. Boulder, Calhan, Caliche, Fowler, Fruita Monument and Machebeuf (which ran off the state's longest winning streak, male or female, at 72 consecutive victories) each has three titles.

New statistics have emerged with the advent of girls basketball in Colorado. Only 11 schools have brought home both a boys and a girls championship banner. Leading the way is Merino with seven titles (six boys and one girls). Boulder, whose boys and girls teams have three titles apiece, and Wheat Ridge (four boys and two girls) have won six. Caliche, Eads, Boulder Fairview, Ft. Collins, Fruita Monument, Lutheran and Ponderosa also have won championships in both boys and girls basketball.

__Bert Borgmann__ is the director of media, promotions and marketing for the Colorado High School Activities Association. Before joining the CHSAA, he was director of sports information and promotion at the University of Northern Colorado and assistant sports information director at Colorado State University.

Borgmann, 33, earned his bachelor's degree in technical journalism and public relations at CSU in 1981 and his master's degree in educational administration and sports administration in 1983.

He is married to the former Alexandra Hays and they have one son, Logan.

Littleton High School won the 1989 "AAAA" boys title. Photo courtesy of Bruce Keegan, Ponseigo/Keegan Photography.

Colorado High School Boys Championships, 1922-Present

Air Academy, 1989 "AAA"
Akron, 1960 "A," 1989 "A-I"
Alamosa, 1939 "B," 1989 "A"
Arickaree, 1985, 1986 "A-II"
Arriba, 1935 "C"
Aurora Central, 1985 "AAAA"
Bear Creek, 1974 "AAA"
Bennett, 1951, 1964 "C," 1986, 1987 "A-I"
Boulder, 1945 "A," 1977, 1979 "AAA"
Boulder Fairview, 1981 "AAAA"
Branson, 1967 "A"
Brighton, 1951, 1952, 1954 "A"
Broomfield, 1967 "AA"
Brush, 1962 "A," 1965, 1969, 1974 "AA"
Burlington, 1948 "C"
Caliche, 1981 "A-I"
Carbondale, 1954, 1958, 1959 "C"
Castle Rock, 1943 "B"
Center, 1950 "B"
Cheyenne Wells, 1954, 1955 "B"
Climax, 1932 "C"
Colorado Springs, 1932, 1935 "U"
Crowley County, 1968 "AA"
Delta, 1945 "B"
Denver Christian, 1970, 1978, 1980, 1982, 1983 "AA"
Denver East, 1943 "A," 1951, 1952, 1964, 1965 "AAA"
Denver North, 1927, 1934 "U," 1938 "A"
Denver South, 1928, 1933 "U," 1947 "A," 1955, 1958, 1959, 1970 "AAA"
Durango, 1947 "B"
Eads, 1975 "A"
Eagle Valley, 1985 "A-I"
Eaton, 1964, 1972, 1987 "AA"
Edgewater, 1941, 1952 "B"
Elbert, 1988 "A-II"
Englewood, 1938 "B"
Flagler, 1981, 1982, 1984 "A-II"
Ft. Collins, 1941, 1944, 1945 "A," 1954 "AA"
Ft. Luptin, 1955 "B"
Frederick, 1956 "B"
Fruita Monument, 1985 "AAA"
Galeton, 1961, 1963 "C"
George Washington, 1961 "AAA," 1982, 1986 "AAAA"
Glenwood Springs, 1975, 1979, 1984 "AA"
Granada, 1989 "A-II"
Grand Junction, 1946 "B"
Greeley Central, 1922, 1925 "U," 1956, 1957 "AA," 1959, 1960, 1962, 1981 "AAA"
Green Mountain, 1980 "AAA"
Holly, 1951 "B"
Holy Family, 1976 "AA"
Holyoke, 1984 "A-I"
Ignacio, 1988 "A-I"
Iliff, 1973 "A"
Jefferson, 1957, 1959 "A"
Joes, 1929, 1930 "U"
Thomas Jefferson, 1967 "AAA"
Johnstown, 1958 "B"
La Junta, 1949 "B", 1963 "AA"
Lakewood, 1948 "B"
Lamar, 1961 "AA"
Las Animas, 1942 "B," 1955 "A," 1958, 1959 "AA"
Leadville, 1956 "A"
Limon, 1959, 1961, 1962, 1964 "B"
Littleton, 1960 "AA," 1987, 1989 "AAAA"
Longmont, 1937 "U," 1942 "A"
Loveland, 1986 "AAA"
Lutheran, 1985, 1986 "AA"
Manitou Springs, 1975 "AA"
Manual, 1940, 1948, 1949 "A," 1950, 1955 "AA," 1972, 1976 "AAA," 1988 "AAAA"
Mead, 1957 "B"
Merino, 1969, 1970, 1976, 1977, 1978, 1979, 1980 "A"
Middle Park, 1963 "B"
Mitchell, 1971, 1973 "AAA"
Montbello, 1984 "AAAA"
Montezuma-Cortez, 1962 "AA"
Pagosa Springs, 1960 "B"
Peetz, 1962 "B"
Pleasant View, 1946 "C"
Ponderosa, 1988 "AAA"
Pritchett, 1974 "A"
Pueblo Centennial, 1940 "A"
Pueblo Central, 1926, 1931 "U"
Rampart, 1987 "AAA"
Rangeview, 1985 "AAA"
Rocky Ford, 1940 "B"
Rye, 1956 "C," 1982 "A-I"
Salida, 1961 "A," 1964 "AA"
Sanford, 1949, 1950 "C," 1977 "AA"
Silver State Baptist, 1983 "A-I"
Simla, 1983, 1987 "A-II"
Skyline, 1982 "AAA"
Springfield, 1947 "C"
Steamboat Springs, 1971 "AA"
Sterling, 1984 "AAA"
University College, 1936 "U," 1966 "AA"
Walsh, 1948, 1971, 1972 "A"
Wasson, 1978 "AAA"
Weld Central, 1988 "AA"
Weldona, 1960 "C"
Wellington, 1953, 1957 "C"
Westminster, 1950 "A," 1975 "AAA"
Wheat Ridge, 1944 "B," 1955 "A," 1963, 1968 "AAA"
Widefield, 1985 "AAAA"
Wiggins, 1965, 1966 "A"
Windsor, 1923, 1924 "U"
Yuma, 1958, 1963 "A," 1981 "AA"

Colorado High School Girls Basketball Championships, 1976-Present

Arvada West, 1978 "AAA"
Boulder, 1984, 1986, 1989 "AAAA"
Boulder Fairview, 1985 "AAAA"
Calhan, 1977 "A," 1987, 1988 "A-I"
Caliche, 1979 "A," 1981, 1986 "A-I"
Campo, 1976, 1978 "A"
Deer Trail, 1986 "A-II"
Eads, 1981, 1987 "A-II"
Fleming, 1981 "A-II"
Florence, 1983, 1988 "AA"
Ft. Collins, 1983 "AAAA"
Fowler, 1982, 1983, 1989 "A-II"
Fruita Monument, 1981, 1983, 1989 "AAA"
Golden, 1978 "AAA"
Grand Junction, 1984 "AAA"
Lutheran, 1985 "AA"
Machebeuf, 1981, 1982, 1986 "AA"
Merino, 1980 "A-II"
Montrose, 1986 "AAA"
Northglenn, 1987 "AAAA"
Norwood, 1983 "A-II"
Plateau Valley, 1980 "A"
Platte Valley, 1987 "AA"
Ponderosa, 1986 "AAA"
Pueblo South, 1979 "AAA"
Ridgeway, 1982 "A-II"
Roaring Fork, 1984, 1989 "AA"
Sangre de Cristo, 1984 "A-I," 1985 "A-II"
Stratton, 1988 "A-II"
Thompson Valley, 1987, 1988 "AAA"
Thornton, 1988 "AAAA"
Trinidad, 1980 "AA"
Wheat Ridge, 1977 "AAA," 1982 "AAAA"
Wray, 1976, 1977, 1978, 1979 "AA," 1985 "A-I"

MILE HIGH CLASSIC

DON HINCHEY

Some great sporting events don't seem to have ever been born. Like Topsy, and the crabgrass that accompanies spring baseball, they seem to have "just growed." Think of the World Series, the Super Bowl or college basketball's Final Four. Given the huge followings, the great hoopla, and the colossal media coverage that these events now command, it's hard to imagine a time when things could have possibly been otherwise.

But each event had a beginning, and, at least in a couple of cases, it was rather humble.

Take the World Series. In 1903, when the fall classic was first played, major league baseball was comprised of 11 cities and 16 teams. Only one of those towns — St. Louis — was west of the Mississippi River. And when the Boston Red Sox of the upstart American League, founded in 1901, defeated the Pittsburgh Pirates of the established National League, which dated back to 1876, five games to three, it so embarrassed the senior circuit that the Series wasn't held in 1904. The games resumed under new rules in 1905.

One of those 1903 games in Boston did draw 19,000 fans, but national press coverage was almost nonexistent. For example, the Sunday, October 4 *New York Times* had a paltry six column inches on the contest on page four of the sports section — far less and far later than that day's coverage of horse racing, college football, billiards and trap shooting. Even English cricket scores got more ink.

When the national collegiate basketball championship was first played 50 years ago, it wasn't called the Final Four. It was more like the "elemental eight" thanks to the number of teams in the tournament. The total *tournament* attendance in 1939 was 15,025 — less than 3 percent of what it is today — and only 5,500 fans showed up for the title game at Patten Gymnasium in Evanston, Illinois. Quite a contrast to the more than 39,000 fans who watched the 1989 Final Four at the Kingdome in Seattle.

Even the Super Bowl — that throwback to the pomp and pageantry of ancient Rome — made a relatively mild impact, at least by its current standards, when it debuted at the L.A. Coliseum 22 years ago. Fans and sportswriters, alike, had difficulty deciphering its true role in the pantheon of sports events. Entire days would go by without anything being written or said about the game in the media — something unheard of in today's Circus Maximus atmosphere.

Given this perspective, it's a lot easier to have patience with "maturing" sports events, those that are just getting up on their feet, especially when they lack the national attendance and media clout that The Big Three have.

The Mile High Classic is a good example. Unlike Topsy, it had a very definite birth, at least in the mind of Roger Kinney, general chairman of the Denver Organizing Committee. He saw it as a wonderful opportunity to promote college basketball in the metro

With the Mile High Classic basic format established and the inclusion of a Division II game and a childrens' basketball clinic, the Classic was up on it feet.

Denver area and to give regional schools such as Colorado State University, Wyoming and the University of Colorado a chance to show off their programs.

In 1987, the Classic's inaugural year, those goals were partly fulfilled. A 7-0 start by Wyoming, led by Eric Leckner and the irrepressible Fennis Dembo, helped the Cowboys draw attention to themselves and the Classic. The games were played at the Denver Coliseum in late December and despite a bad snowstorm and some stiff TV competition from the University of Wyoming football team — which was inconsiderate enough to be playing in the Holiday Bowl that evening — attendance totaled more than 8,000.

For a while, it seemed as if all 8,000 were Wyoming fans, as the Cowboys lived up to their No. 5 national ranking in the first game of the Division I doubleheader. Despite Benny Dees' frequent substitutions, the Cowboys crushed Cincinnati, 100-73. Leckner dominated the boards, while Dembo's court antics and fine shooting delighted the fans. But it was reserve guard Reggie Fox who walked away with MVP honors, as he scored a game-high 26 points and put in three of four from three-point range.

In the nightcap, a gutsy, but outgunned, Colorado team, led by senior Scott Wilke, lost to Illinois, 86-68. The Buffs started poorly and were down by as many as 18 points in the middle of the first half. But with five minutes left in the period, they staged a 16-4 rally to pull within six. After that, however, it was all Illinois as Lou Henson's team harassed and out-hustled Colorado, forcing 24 Buff turnovers. Backup forward Lowell Hamilton was a leader in that department, earning MVP honors for his efforts.

The first Mile High Classic was by no means a mega-event, probably due to the venue and the fact that the games were blowouts. But as Kinney would often say, "You gotta walk before you can run." With the basic format in place and the inclusion of a Division II game — Metro State beat Colorado Baptist — and a childrens' basketball clinic, the Classic was up on its feet and headed in the right direction.

In 1988, it started to jog. For starters, the games were moved to McNichols Sports Arena, which not only had four locker rooms — the Coliseum had only two — but also more seats and better sight lines. None of the four Division I teams was nationally ranked, but they did provide some interesting match-ups. To add a little spice to the pot, a Division II tournament was included.

In the first game of the Division I doubleheader, a young — and, at times, sloppy — Wyoming team gave Wake Forest of the Atlantic Coast Conference all it could handle at both ends of the court. It was fast-break, in-your-face basketball for 40 minutes. But Bob Staak and his Demon Deacons, led by Sam "Poison" Ivy, kept their composure and held on to beat the Cowboys, 82-77. Wyoming's Robyn Davis led all scorers with 27 points and

The Classic began to jog in 1988 when the games were moved to McNichols Sports Arena featuring adequate locker facilities, more seats, better sight lines and continued support from community leaders.

captured the game's MVP award.

In the second game, Colorado again got off to a poor start and seemed to be heading for a beating. Gene Keady's Purdue squad was not the same team that had won its conference title the previous year. But the Boilermakers were big and burly, and they obviously were used to throwing their weight around in the rough-and-tough Big 10. Through 30 minutes, that's exactly what happened. Purdue pushed, shoved and elbowed the Buffaloes all over the court and outshot CU by a wide margin.

But something happened in the last 10 minutes. Maybe the players overheard TV announcer Irv Brown tell his audience when the Buffs were down by 17 points that, "They're not out of it. They could still win this thing." Or maybe they remembered something CU coach Tom Miller told them in their closed shoot-around earlier that day. Whatever it was, the CU players wouldn't give up.

Their tenacity began to tire the Boilermakers, then it tugged at their lead, and finally, it frustrated them. Back-to-back three-point buckets by Reggie Morton and Steve Wise seemed to stun Purdue, and the crowd — asleep throughout the game — suddenly grew vocal, loud and expectant.

As the clock wound down to a minute, the tension rose from the floor to McNichols' roof. Had the Purdue team been tested like this before? Colorado certainly had, losing two of its first four games by one-point margins. CU fans must have been wondering if this would be a continuation of the Buffs' "close-but-no-cigar" theme, or if they would somehow find a way to pull it off. The suspense lasted only 53 more seconds. With seven ticks left on the clock, Reggie Morton pumped in a 15-footer to give Colorado a 67-66 lead and the victory. Shaun Vandiver led the Buffs with 20 points, but it was Reggie Morton who won MVP honors for his iceman-like heroics.

On a somewhat disappointing note, only 7,500 people watched the Division I doubleheader and the Division II tournament, won by Metro State College. On the other hand the games provided an excellent bang for the patrons' entertainment buck and may have served to whet the fans' appetite for future Classic action.

And just what is the future of the Mile High Classic? It's difficult, and perhaps unnecessary, to look past 1989, when the games return to McNichols Arena. For in the third year of the event, the Classic promises to come of age.

First of all, the event will change from a Division I doubleheader format to a two-night tournament. Secondly, the games will once again be played in late December, allowing ample opportunity for proper promotion.

But perhaps most importantly, local fans will get a taste of what they've been clamoring for from the beginning: the chance to watch a national powerhouse. In 1989, Dean Smith will arrive with his University of North Carolina Tarheels. Also playing in the Classic for the first time will be Boyd "Tiny" Grant's

The 1988 Mile High Classic provided an excellent bang for the patrons' entertainment buck and may have served to whet the fans' appetite for future Classic action.

As is seen from these photographs, the 1988 Mile High Classic appealed to and was enjoyed by all segments of the community. All photographs courtesy of Fritz Law.

resurgent CSU Rams, the 1989 WAC champions. This blend of big-time power and local scrapper could provide the Classic with enough appeal to push attendance past the 10,000 mark.

Another trump card in the Classic's future is the 1990 Final Four, which Denver will host for the first time. Can the Classic borrow some charisma from that event to help it become a local staple? Will the Final Four trigger the kind of regional enthusiasm necescessary to bolster local basketball programs and sustain the Classic in years to come? It's hard to predict. The lineup will certainly help build local awareness and excitement, and it might even boost attendance.

But perhaps its greatest legacy will be the recognition that sports events aren't "born" with super status. They require support, cooperation, patience and some intelligent tinkering. Then, if they're lucky, someday somebody may say, "Heck, they just growed."

Don Hinchey *was born and raised on the south side of Chicago. He attended the University of Northern Colorado on a wrestling scholarship and graduated in 1971 with a degree in English education.*

After college, Hinchey held a variety of jobs, including stints in retail sales, construction and tire warehousing. For the past five years, he has served in executive capacities for the Denver Baseball Commission, the Denver Organizing Committee and the Greater Denver Chamber of Commerce.

He has edited two books — one on contract bridge and the other a biography of industrialist Henry J. Kaiser.

Hinchey, 41, and his wife Marcia have three children: Adam, Laura and Mark. The family lives in Lakewood.

This team from Colorado State University won the 1989 Western Athletic Conference championship. Photo courtesy of CSU's Sports Information Department.

Alabama and North Carolina State battle at the 1985 NCAA West Regional Tournament at McNichols Sports Arena. Photo courtesy of Rich Clarkson/Sports Illustrated.

Rocky Mountain News
NCAA
ALABAMA
23
NCAA Radio Net

1985 & 1989 NCAA WEST REGIONALS

B.G. BROOKS

*Denver's McNichols Sports Arena hosts a variety of sporting events. Photo courtesy of The Denver Nuggets. Opposite: When the national collegiate basketball championship was first played 50 years ago, the media barely noticed. Media attention has increased considerably as seen here at the 1989 NCAA West Regional Tournament at McNichols in Denver. Photo courtesy of Rich Clarkson/*Sports Illustrated.

Although 1990 marks Denver's first time as host for a Final Four, the Mile High City has recently become a familiar stop on the increasingly glitzy pathway to the NCAA Championship.

Denver's McNichols Sports Arena has been the site of two of the past five NCAA West Regionals, which in 1985 and 1989 gave the city an enticing glimpse of what awaits this spring — albeit on a much grander scale.

The 1985 West Regional was considered a rehearsal for '89 and '90, but there weren't many major glitches in the local production company's show.

Said Cedrick Dempsey, Arizona's athletic director and then a member of the West Regional site selection committee: "I'd give it a very solid 'A.' I think the way it was all set up exceeded everyone's expectations . . . . I think even the eastern teams were beginning to feel comfortable in the West."

Indeed, in 1985, one of the eastern entries — St. John's University of New York — found considerable comfort and success in the Mountain Time Zone. Four years later, another eastern entry — Seton Hall — would, too.

Fueled by a dream-wrecker and zone-breaker named Chris Mullin, Lou Carnesecca's St. John's Redmen swept past Kentucky, 86-70, in the Friday night semifinals in what would be Joe B. Hall's final game as the Wildcats' coach.

The 56-year-old Hall, enjoying a Denver homecoming of sorts (he coached at Regis College), announced his retirement to the Bluegrass faithful during his postgame radio show. He cited his age as one reason for stepping down, which puzzled the 60-year-old Carnesecca.

"It's a sad commentary that Joe B. Hall believes 56 is old for a coach," Carnesecca said. "I don't know what his other reasons are; they're his own. But this is one of the most successful basketball coaches in the country. It's awfully hard to lose one of his caliber."

Perhaps Hall's aging process accelerated after witnessing Mullin's marksmanship.

"Tonight," said Mullin after he'd scored 30 points, "I had probably the easiest shots I've gotten all year. Kentucky didn't change their game plan [of collapsing on the Redmen big men]. They didn't come out too much, and I was kind of relieved, really. It was like being let out of jail for a night."

And Mullin's weekend pass in the Rockies continued. Two afternoons later, he and the Redmen answered every North Carolina State challenge, dispatching the Wolfpack, 69-60, and rewarding Carnesecca with his first trip to the Final Four.

Mullin did everything he could to make sure it happened. Alternately shooting his soft left-handed jumpers and slicing to the basket, the college Player of the Year scored 25 points.

A three-minute sequence late in the game encapsulated Mullin's championship contributions: NC State had closed to 43-42 on Lorenzo Charles' four consecutive free throws.

10:38
Pana
9 NEWS

*Seton Hall's Pete Carlessimo arrived in Denver for the West Regionals as the youngest and most unheralded member of the coaching quartet. At the tournament's conclusion, Carlessimo and his talented Pirates were strangers to no one. Photo courtesy of Rich Clarkson/***Sports Illustrated***.*

St. John's misfired on its next possession, but the ever-alert Mullin picked up the loose ball rebound and, in the same motion, buried a baseline jumper. Moments later, he hit a pair of free throws and the Redmen led, 47-42. The Wolfpack wouldn't get within three points the rest of the game.

"St. John's just had a response for everything we threw at them. And that's why they won," said NC State's head coach, Jim Valvano, whose team had ousted Alabama, 61-55, to reach the West title game.

Afterward, the normally loquacious Carnesecca slipped out of character: "It's very difficult for me to express myself. I'm usually very verbal. With five seconds left in the game, I looked up at the clock and kept thinking, 'We're going, we're going.'"

Four seasons later, another eastern coach came west and enjoyed the same experience.

In 1989, Seton Hall's Pete Carlessimo arrived in Denver as the youngest and most unheralded member of a colorful and successful coaching quartet. At the West Regional's conclusion, Carlessimo and his talented and defensively driven Pirates were strangers to no one.

The other West Regional coaches — Indiana's Bobby Knight, Arizona's Lute Olson and Nevada-Las Vegas' Jerry Tarkanian — weren't surprised by Seton Hall's success, or by Carlessimo's penchant for pushing all the right strategical buttons during a game.

The Pirates, a collection of mostly anonymous Easterners with a couple of international players (Australia's Andrew Gaze and Puerto Rico's Ramon Ramos) spicing the mix, dispatched second-seeded Indiana with surprising ease, 78-65, in their first game.

It would be the last college game for Jay Edwards, the sophomore guard who had become the Hoosiers' Mr. Clutch thanks to his game-winning, last-second shots during Big Ten play. After scoring only two first-half points, Edwards finished with 18. A couple of weeks later, he announced he would make himself eligible for the NBA draft.

"I felt Seton Hall had the stronger team, and I told PJ that after the game," Knight said.

Carlessimo didn't disagree: "We won because we had better players — and more of them."

Knight, who can be as charming as he can be irascible, was on his best behavior in Denver. Early on during his western weekend, he left the media laughing by likening himself to Santa Claus, saying he and Claus were both "just old, overweight guys that kids love."

But the stately Olson, who'd watched his Wildcats stay at or near the No. 1 spot nationally through much of the season, wasn't in a jovial mood before the game with the Runnin' Rebels. Afterward, his mood worsened.

With four seconds to play, UNLV's Anderson Hunt buried a three-pointer from the right wing to beat the top-seeded Wildcats, 68-67. Arizona was stunned, and so, it seemed, was a local reporter who asked a somber Olson if he would characterize the loss as "bitter."

Olson grinned incredulously, then asked for a show of hands in the interview room. "How many of you think this could be called a bitter loss? It ends our season, so sure, it's bitter. We were just one point shy of sitting here talking about what a great offensive job we did down the stretch."

But more and more, "great defensive jobs" in the NCAA tournament were becoming Seton Hall's trademark. The West Regional championship matched the Runnin' Rebels' speed and quickness against the Pirates' depth and strength inside.

UNLV could hardly be called a physically imposing team, and the raccoon-eyed Tarkanian acknowledged it: "We're probably the skinniest team in the country, but I like our toughness."

Yet he didn't like what he saw in the championship game. And as for toughness in the final half, well, 'Vegas crapped out.

The Runnin' Rebels stayed close for 20 minutes, trailing by only four, 34-30, at halftime. That, in itself, was startling, because UNLV was frigid, hitting just 29% of its shots.

". . . We caused so many turnovers [12] we stayed in it," offered Tarkanian. "But it seemed like all of a sudden in the second half, there was nothing left in us. They played for 40 minutes, we played for 30. They certainly whipped us good."

The most telling part of the whipping came during a 14-0 Seton Hall run that produced a 60-45 lead with just under 10 minutes to play. Gaze, the 6'7" Aussie called "Jack" by his teammates, hit five of his game-high 19 points and blocked a shot during that surge.

The Rundown Rebels wilted and died.

And for the first time, ever, "The Hall" was on its way to the Final Four and a chance at the NCAA Championship.

*Coach Joe B. Hall announced his retirement following the defeat of his Kentucky Wildcats by St. John's in the 1985 NCAA West Regional semifinal. Photo courtesy of Rich Clarkson/***Sports Illustrated***.*

***B.G. Brooks** has worked for the* Rocky Mountain News *for the past 11 years. Hired to cover the Denver Broncos in 1978, Brooks followed the National Football League team for the next three seasons. He also was the News' sports editor from 1979-1984, then worked as the newspaper's NFL at-large writer in 1985 before returning to the Broncos beat in 1986. He has covered college athletics, primarily the University of Colorado, since 1987.*

Brooks, 42, is a 1970 graduate of Memphis State University. Before joining the News, he worked for the Memphis Commercial Appeal, *the* Columbia Daily Tribune *and* The Columbia Missourian.

Brooks and his wife, Patti, have two children, Brian, 14, and Kelley, 11. They live in Broomfield.

SOMEPLACE NEAR DENVER - 1990
WHY THEY REALLY CHOSE THE MILE HIGH CITY TO HOST THE FINAL FOUR
YOU'RE KIDDING, RIGHT?
NO... HONEST. GOD WANTED A CLOSER SEAT.
MENU
drew litton
ROCKY MOUNTAIN NEWS

*"It's my favorite event. There is still nothing quite like that first day when all . . . teams are participating, the bands and the cheerleaders are going and the crowd is all excited. Nothing like it."— Irv Brown. Photo courtesy of Rich Clarkson/*Sports Illustrated.

DENVER NUGGETS

TOM HOHENSEE

A professional basketball team destined to play its home games in a vibrant young city nestled in the foothills of the Rocky Mountains was born more than 20 years ago. At the time, they were known as the Rockets, and when they played their first home game at Denver's Auditorium Arena on October 15, 1967, a crowd of 2,748 fans looked on as the locals bested the Anaheim Amigos, 110-105, in the first American Basketball Association contest ever held in the Mile High City.

From those rather humble beginnings have risen today's Denver Nuggets, a proud National Basketball Association franchise that plays its home contests in McNichols Sports Arena, one of the finest basketball facilities in the United States. In their first 22 seasons of action, the Rockets/Nuggets have won 988 regular-season games. Those triumphs have resulted in one ABA regular-season title, two ABA division titles and four NBA division championships. The team has won nearly 55 percent of its games during that time, a mark of consistency that stands as a tribute to the players and management that have represented Denver during more than two decades of excitement.

More than 10 million fans have witnessed Rockets/Nuggets basketball games in the Auditorium Arena and McNichols Arena during this 22-year period. And while cynics may complain that the franchise has yet to bring a playoff title to the Rocky Mountain region, the fans who appreciate the skills and talents of professional basketball players have certainly received their money's worth in thrills since the sport arrived here in 1967.

The early Rockets may not have been immediately embraced by Denver's sports fans, but the team did enjoy success on the floor almost from the outset. The Rockets averaged 47 wins during their first three seasons in the ABA, and they captured the league's Western Division title in 1969-70. Those early teams were led by three-time All-ABA choice Larry Jones, but it wasn't until Spencer Haywood came along that the divisional title was won. The former Olympic standout was the League's MVP and Rookie of the Year in his lone season as a Rocket, and many of his game and single-season records still stand in the Denver record book.

The early 1970s weren't prosperous years for the franchise, despite guard Ralph Simpson's heroics. By 1973-74, attendance was on the wane, and some thought the franchise was on the verge of extinction. Thus, the stage was set for some radical changes that would drastically alter the fortunes of pro basketball in Denver.

The move that set off a chain reaction of success came in June of 1974 when Carl Scheer was hired as the club's new president and general manager. A two-time ABA Executive of the Year with the Carolina Cougars, Scheer changed the franchise's image. He gave the club a new nickname, a new logo, new team colors and a new lease on life. Within months of his arrival,

One of the Nuggets' superstars is Alex English, the silky smooth forward whose soft-spoken manner and gentle off the court nature belie his toughness on the floor. The Nuggets' all-time scoring leader, English set a new NBA record in 1988-89 by scoring more than 2,000 points in a single season for the eighth consecutive year.

Carl Scheer was hired in June of 1974 as the club's new president and general manager. Scheer brought honor and glory to the Mile High City in 1984 by bringing the 1984 NBA All-Star Game to McNichols, and he was the mastermind behind the first All-Star Saturday.

the Denver Nuggets became a hot sports property, and, once again, it soon became fashionable to be a pro basketball fan in the Mile High City.

One of Scheer's first and most significant moves was hiring Larry Brown as head coach. The former North Carolina and ABA star quickly assembled a hustling young team that captured the hearts of Denver sports fans. The 1974-75 Nuggets rolled to a 65-19 record, and their remarkable turnaround on the court was reflected at the turnstiles as 29 sellout crowds jammed tiny Auditorium Arena.

Scheer still harbors fond memories of that first season in Denver.

"It was truly marvelous to watch that team overachieve its way to 65 wins," he remembers. "They played so hard every night that the fans fell in love with them, and they transformed the old Arena from a morgue to a death pit for visiting teams. No one could beat us at home, and the fans loved it. Still, I don't know if that season is as memorable as the one that followed it."

What followed in 1975-76 was possibly the most memorable season in the history of the franchise, and it's still one that many Denver fans recall with a special feeling. For one thing, it marked the opening of McNichols Sports Arena, and the Nuggets smashed every ABA attendance record as they roared to 60 wins and the regular-season title.

Led by Rookie of the Year David Thompson, as well as Dan Issel and Bobby Jones, the Nuggets advanced to the 1976 ABA playoff finals against Julius Erving and the New York Nets. The Nuggets lost in six games in a series that featured Thompson and Erving, the league's two marquee players, in a shootout that will never be forgotten. It was a fine finish for a league that brought the excitement of professional basketball to areas that the NBA had previously overlooked.

Also memorable from that final ABA season was the league's 1976 All-Star Game at McNichols Arena. A record crowd turned out to see the Nuggets beat the ABA All-Stars, thanks to an MVP performance by Thompson. The night also included a halftime slam dunk contest that saw Erving build his legend as he dazzled the fans and his competitors with some unforgettable athletic feats.

"It was one of those nights you never wanted to come to an end," recalls Scheer.

The ABA came to an end shortly after the Nuggets-Nets championship series, but Denver was one of four cities brought into the NBA as part of a merger plan that included a significant measure of input from Scheer. Thus, in just two years, he had taken a dying franchise in a dying league and given it new life in the major league of professional basketball.

Rookie of the Year David Thompson, with Dan Issel and Bobby Jones led the Nuggets to the 1976 ABA playoff finals against the New York Nets.

Many NBA skeptics doubted the strength of the ABA transplants, but the Nuggets immediately established themselves as a power, and Denver fans enabled the franchise to lead the league in attendance in each of its first two campaigns. Those enthusiastic crowds saw their heroes win back-to-back Midwest Division titles, and save for a few years, the Nuggets have been consistently competitive in their 13 NBA seasons.

Carl Scheer departed Denver after the 1983-84 season, a disappointing year for the Nuggets. Even in his final year, however, Scheer brought honor and glory to the Mile High City. He managed to bring the 1984 NBA All-Star Game to McNichols, and he was the mastermind behind the first All-Star Saturday. The NBA's first slam-dunk contest and old-timers game were held in Denver that year, and since then, the All-Star Weekend has become the league's biggest promotional activity of each calendar year.

The Nuggets of the 1980s have largely been coach Doug Moe's teams, and that has meant

The Nuggets' precursor, the Rockets, were led to the league's Western Division title in 1969-70 by Spencer Haywood, a former Olympic standout and MVP and Rookie of the Year in his lone season with the Rockets.

Among the Nuggets' outstanding players, the first who comes to mind is Dan Issel, the consummate pro who closed out his career with more than 27,000 points, among the highest totals in pro basketball history.

the most exciting brand of basketball in the NBA. While they've never been blessed with enough talent to win a championship, Moe's clubs have consistently won with a combination of his fast-paced, uptempo offense, a harassing pressure defense, and a mental toughness that has allowed them to beat opponents considered vastly superior in ability.

Moe has gotten much of the credit for his team's accomplishments, but he would be the first to point out that his clubs have not been devoid of outstanding players. The first who comes to mind is Dan Issel, the consummate pro. The "Horse" closed out his career with more than 27,000 points, among the highest totals in pro basketball history, and he was unquestionably the most popular player in franchise history.

Moe's other superstar has been Alex English, the silky smooth forward whose soft-spoken manner and gentle off the court nature belie his toughness on the floor. The Nuggets' all-time scoring leader who's picked up most of his points with a feathery touch around the basket, English set a new NBA record in 1988-89 by scoring more than 2,000 points in a single season for the eighth consecutive year.

Issel's jersey now hangs from the rafters of McNichols Arena, and English's is sure to follow once he retires. Others also have contributed to Denver's success in the 1980s. Kiki Vandeweghe combined with Issel and English to help the Nuggets establish numerous NBA scoring records early in the decade, and two of the players obtained from Portland in a 1984 trade for Vandeweghe — Fat Lever and Calvin Natt — also have achieved star status.

Two players obtained from Portland in a 1984 trade included Fat Lever and Calvin Natt who have achieved star status with the Nuggets. Here Lever goes for a basket in a game against Cleveland.

In 1974, one of Scheer's first and most significant moves was to hire Larry Brown as head coach. Brown quickly assembled a hustling young team that captured the hearts of Denver sports fans.

One of the things that's made Moe's clubs so fascinating has been the emergence of role players who have far surpassed the expectations most people held for them. Three-point shooters such as Michael Adams and Mike Evans, defensive specialists such as T.R. Dunn, and kamikaze types such as Bill Hanzlik and Glen Gondrezick all have made Nuggets teams fun to watch, as well as surprisingly competitive.

Denver's pro basketball success has resulted from a combination of elements. Players, coaches and front office executives have all played major roles in this success story, and names such as Issel, English, Thompson, Moe, Brown, Scheer, Byron Beck, Vince Boryla, Red McCombs, Sidney Shlenker and Pete Babcock will long be prominent in the city's pro basketball annals.

But the real secret to the Denver Nuggets' success goes beyond a few marquee names. There's a spirit here that's unique to professional sports organizations. And even though that spirit hasn't led to a string of championships, it has resulted in a tradition of hustle, hard work and excitement. That tradition has been more than enough to make the Denver Nuggets one of professional basketball's blue chip franchises.

The Nuggets of the 1980s have largely been coach Doug Moe's teams, and that has meant the most exciting brand of basketball in the NBA. All photos courtesy of Bill Young/The Denver Nuggets and Tom Hohensee.

Now in his fourth year as a media manager in the field marketing department at the Coors Brewing Co. in Golden, **Tom Hohensee** *moved to Colorado in 1978 to be the public relations director for the Denver Nuggets, a job he held for seven years.*

Born and reared in Buffalo, New York, Hohensee earned a bachelor's degree in journalism from St. Bonaventure University and a master's degree in radio/television from Syracuse University before enlisting in the U.S. Army in 1968.

After his discharge, Hohensee was a radio news and sports announcer before becoming the news bureau director at Niagara University in 1974.

He lives in Aurora with his wife, Shary, and their three children — Tom, Brenda and Mike.

When a high school guard sprained an ankle, we treated him like a Bronco.

When Brad Moody hurt his ankle during practice with the Golden High Demons, they said he'd be out the rest of the season. On crutches.

But Brad came to the AMI/Denver Broncos Sports Medicine Center. We treated him the same way we would treat a Bronco. With state-of-the-art equipment, techniques and exercises.

And in just 3 weeks, Brad was back on the court, shooting for the State Playoffs.

If you have a sports injury, we'll treat you like a Bronco too. With a personalized treatment and rehabilitation program developed by our staff of sports injury experts. Like Steve Antonopulos, Head Athletic Trainer of the Denver Broncos. Plus a team of physical therapists specially trained in sports medicine.

And every one of your workouts will be individually supervised. And carefully monitored.

Whether or not you're a professional athlete, if you have an injury you need professional attention. So ask your doctor about the Sports Medicine Centers, or call the center nearest you.

At the AMI/Denver Broncos Sports Medicine Centers, you don't have to be a Demon. Or a Bronco. But we'll treat you like one.

Wheat Ridge • 70 Executive Center # 1 • 4891 Independence • 425-8838
AMI Healthcare Plaza-Centennial • 14200 E. Arapahoe Road and Jordan • 699-3075
Look for our new Thornton center opening in the fall.

Boys Clubs of Metro Denver, Inc.

"Making the future happen for over 7000 boys per year"

TRIBUNE
GCHS
32-33
VISITORS
TRIBUNE
158
415
Undefeated
Credit: Denver Public Library Western History Dept. Photo by Eagan
TEAMWORK
Everyone knows that getting to the top takes hard work. But getting to the top and staying there takes more—teamwork.
At Capitol, we know you must give 110% of yourself to stay above the competition. Each and every member of our team is a seasoned graphic arts veteran who knows what it takes to get the job done and does it.
So, if what you want is a team of professionals dedicated to providing the finest product possible, call us. Let our team work for you.
CAPITOL
ENGRAVING
Graphic Specialists
Color Separation • Digital Prepress
1463 W. Alameda Ave. Denver, CO 80223
(303) 777-7550 1-800-634-1564
DENVER • PHOENIX • SALT LAKE CITY

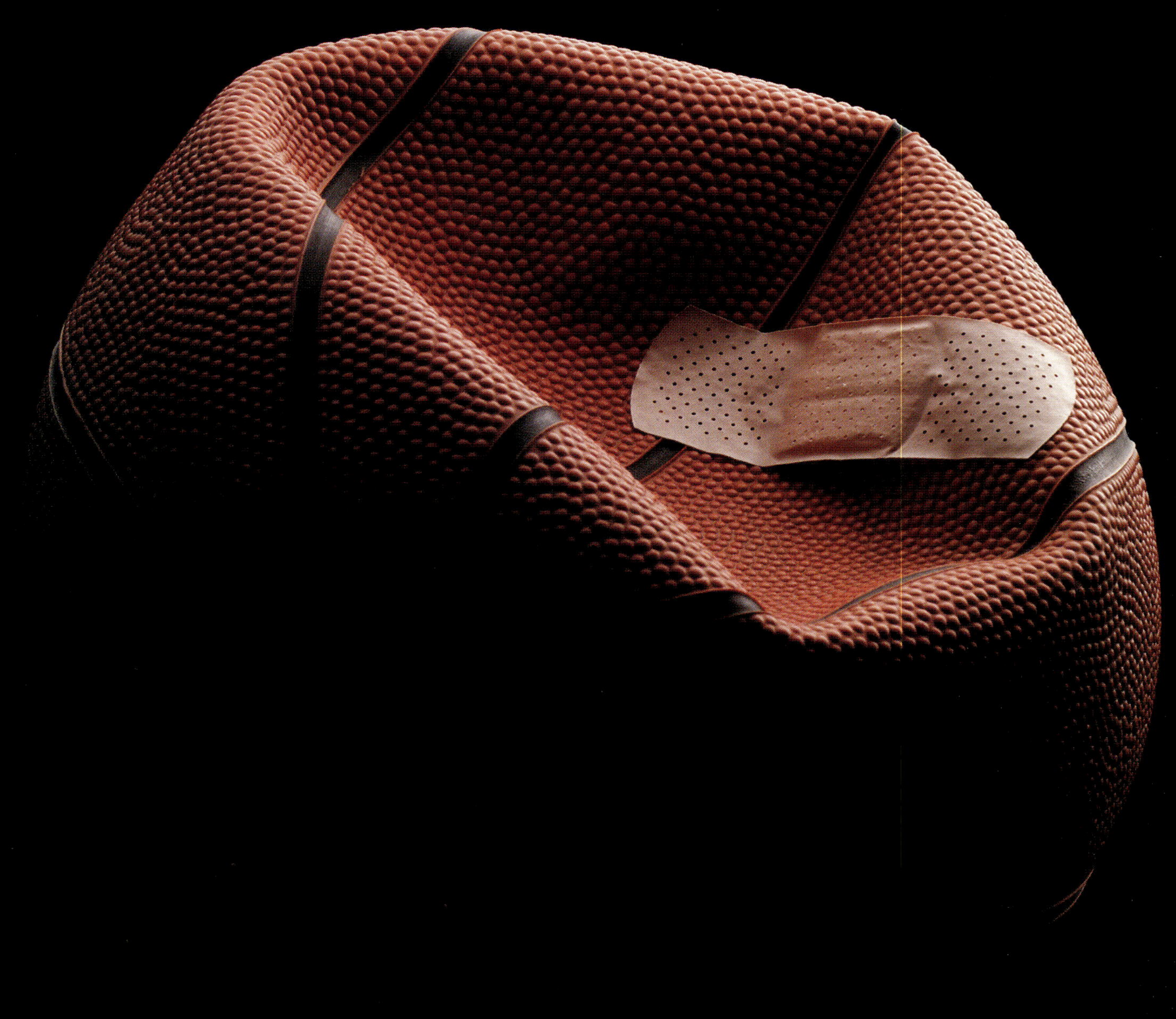
TO STAY IN THE GAME,
YOU HAVE TO STAY HEALTHY.
At Comprecare, our high quality, comprehensive health coverage is helping to keep over 175,000 members across Colorado in the game. And not on the bench.
COMPRECARE
Feels So Much Better

ALL-
STARS
Coors
EXTRA GOLD
Draft
A full-bodied, robust beer.
Coors
Brewed in a Tradition of Excellence
Since 1873
Coors
LIGHT
BEER
Contains only natural ingredients
with no preservatives or additives.
12 Fluid Ounces (355ml)
DRINK
SAFELY
©1989 Coors Brewing Company, Golden, Colorado 80401 • Brewer of Fine Quality Beers Since 1873.8374

THE BEST RECEPTION YOU'LL EVER GET.

We welcome the nation's finest college athletes to Denver for the NCAA "Final-Four" Tournament.

We are proud to tell you that Denver has played a dramatic role in bringing the excitement of college basketball to people throughout the nation.

Thanks to cable pioneer Bill Daniels, Denver has become the "cable television capital of the country." The companies based right here decide what kind of programming will be shown to cable subscribers all across America. Their support for sports means more college basketball games than ever before are being televised throughout the nation. And, cable is delivering those games to many who otherwise would not be able to enjoy them.

America wins thanks to cable television. And, may the best team win the NCAA Championship.

DANIELS
&ASSOCIATES

3200 Cherry Creek South Drive, Suite 500, Denver, Colorado 80209, (303) 778-5555. New York Office: 299 Park Avenue, New York, New York 10171, (212) 935-5900.
Daniels & Associates is a member of the National Association of Securities Dealers Inc. and all its professional personnel are licensed with the NASD.

The Denver Athletic Club

Since 1884

Rocky Mountain Basketball

Since 1893

Traditions of Sporting Excellence

$13/square foot.

Right now, your business can get a home on the range for a song.

Metro Denver's average cost for prime office space is only about $13 per square foot. Compare that to $41 in Boston, $38 in Chicago, $30 in Los Angeles, and $23 in Seattle.

You'll find similar savings on warehouse and manufacturing space, too—but you should move fast because rates are on their way up.

You'll also find a workforce that's 63% above the national average in college-educated adults. And a community that's investing $3 billion in what will be the world's largest international airport.

With numbers like that, Denver is every inch a bottom-line value and a golden opportunity.

Playground included.

Photo Credit: Andrew Photography/Keystone Resort

Of course, the numbers only begin to tell Denver's story.

Look closer and you'll see the rest written in sunny days (300 a year), a surprisingly mild climate and an active lifestyle.

The Rockies west of Denver are a playground of world-class ski areas, national parks and dazzling scenery. Colorado also has more golf courses per capita than any other state.

It's a built-in benefits package that makes recruiting and keeping good people easy.

To get a closer look at Denver, call the Metro Denver Network today: (303) 894-8500.

Denver.

Take a closer look.

NCAA FINAL FOUR
1990
IN 1990, COLLEGE BASKETBALL
WILL RISE TO NEW HEIGHTS.
The mile-high city of Denver, host of the 1990 NCAA Final Four, can't wait to welcome you.

WE'RE SO BIG, WE COULD HOST THE SWEET 16

AND THE FINAL FOUR

SIMULTANEOUSLY.

We're not a sports complex, however. With 162,200 square feet, we're the largest merchandise mart/trade show/special event facility in the entire Rocky Mountain area.

If you have an event coming up (big or small), consider holding it at the Denver Merchandise Mart. We offer a total package of unmatched facilities, the most experienced staff, and a long list of services.

Last year, we hosted over 150 events – events that ran smoothly because our people are specialists who know that little details can make all the difference.

We can provide freight services, registration services, set-up services, catering services (for up to 4,000 people), security services, and every other service needed for a successful show.

The Mart is also recognized as the premier wholesale marketplace for the region's gift, apparel, and western goods retailers. Thousands of buyers – some from around the world – attend trade shows held in the permanent showrooms headquartered at the Mart and in our exhibition facilities.

Our location at I-25 and 58th Avenue means we're easy to reach. And our 3,000 free parking spaces are appreciated by all who attend our events.

Why do so many organizations in the Rocky Mountain and Central Plains Regions count on us? Because we don't drop the ball.

For more information, please call or write.

DENVER MERCHANDISE MART

451 E. 58th Ave. / Denver, Colorado 80216 / (303) 292-MART

The Rocky Mountain's Leading Sporting Goods Stores

With a Growing Kingdom of Sportscastles!

▲ Denver Sportscastle

▲ Salt Lake City Sportscastle

Brand NEW Kansas City Sportscastle!

NOW OPEN! Too New to View!

▲ Kansas City Sportscastle

Brand NEW St. Louis Sportscastle!

NOW OPEN! Too New to View!

St. Louis Sportscastle ▶

4 Incredible Sportscastles and 70 Locations! Featuring:
• Cameras • Skis • Ski Clothing • Footwear • Sportswear •
• Bicycling • Backpacking • Camping • Golf • Tennis •
• Fitness Equipment • Athletics • More!

Stores throughout the West!

Colorado . Utah . Wyoming . Missouri

Like The Final Four— We Provide The Best Performance In The Construction Industry!

Tabor Center

Stapleton International Airport

Colorado Convention Center

Fine Typography,
Camera Production
and Desktop
produced with creative
and technical
excellence to meet the
highest standards of
Denver's graphic
community.
For a price quote
or an appointment
with a sales representative
call 698 2125.
Campro
Systems, Ltd.
124 W 5th Ave • Denver, CO • 80204 • 303/698-2125

You can do it all with the wide range of investments available from IDS Financial Services. Creating a balanced portfolio of quality investments should be one of your primary concerns, no matter what your goals are. When you turn to us for financial information and products, you'll find a whole team of professionals ready to coach you point for point.

IDS Financial is known for taking the lead in developing products to meet the needs of even the most demanding clients.

Discover how simple it can be to find investments to help you meet your own objectives. Meet with the investment advisory professionals at Windsor Financial Group or with representatives at other IDS Financial Services offices throughout the country.

As the major player in the game of financial opportunities, you'll want to call your broker or one of our financial advisors at (303) 756-6665 to keep scoring top money investments. Make us part of your winning team.

WINDSOR
FINANCIAL
GROUP

1777 S. Harrison, Suite 420
Denver, CO 80210
303 756-6665

Presley F. Askew
President of
Windsor Financial Group

"You don't win multi-million dollar contracts
on price alone. They've put together the most
advanced network in the world.
"That's a very tough combination to beat."
—telecommunications analyst
MCI. We showed them. Let us show you.®
© MCI Communications Corporation, 1989.
MCI

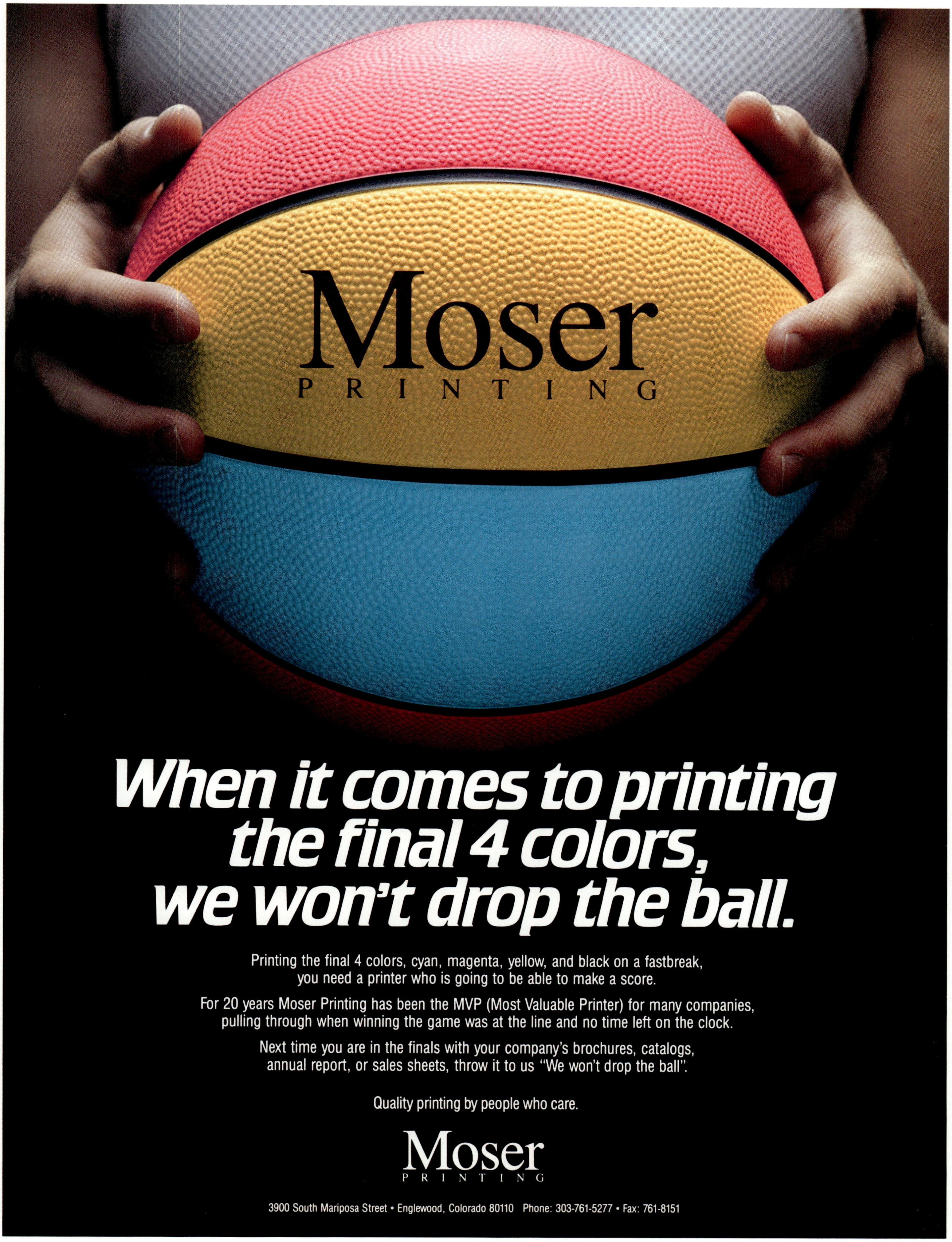
Moser
PRINTING
When it comes to printing the final 4 colors, we won't drop the ball.
Printing the final 4 colors, cyan, magenta, yellow, and black on a fastbreak, you need a printer who is going to be able to make a score.
For 20 years Moser Printing has been the MVP (Most Valuable Printer) for many companies, pulling through when winning the game was at the line and no time left on the clock.
Next time you are in the finals with your company's brochures, catalogs, annual report, or sales sheets, throw it to us "We won't drop the ball".
Quality printing by people who care.
Moser
PRINTING
3900 South Mariposa Street • Englewood, Colorado 80110 Phone: 303-761-5277 • Fax: 761-8151

STRATEGY

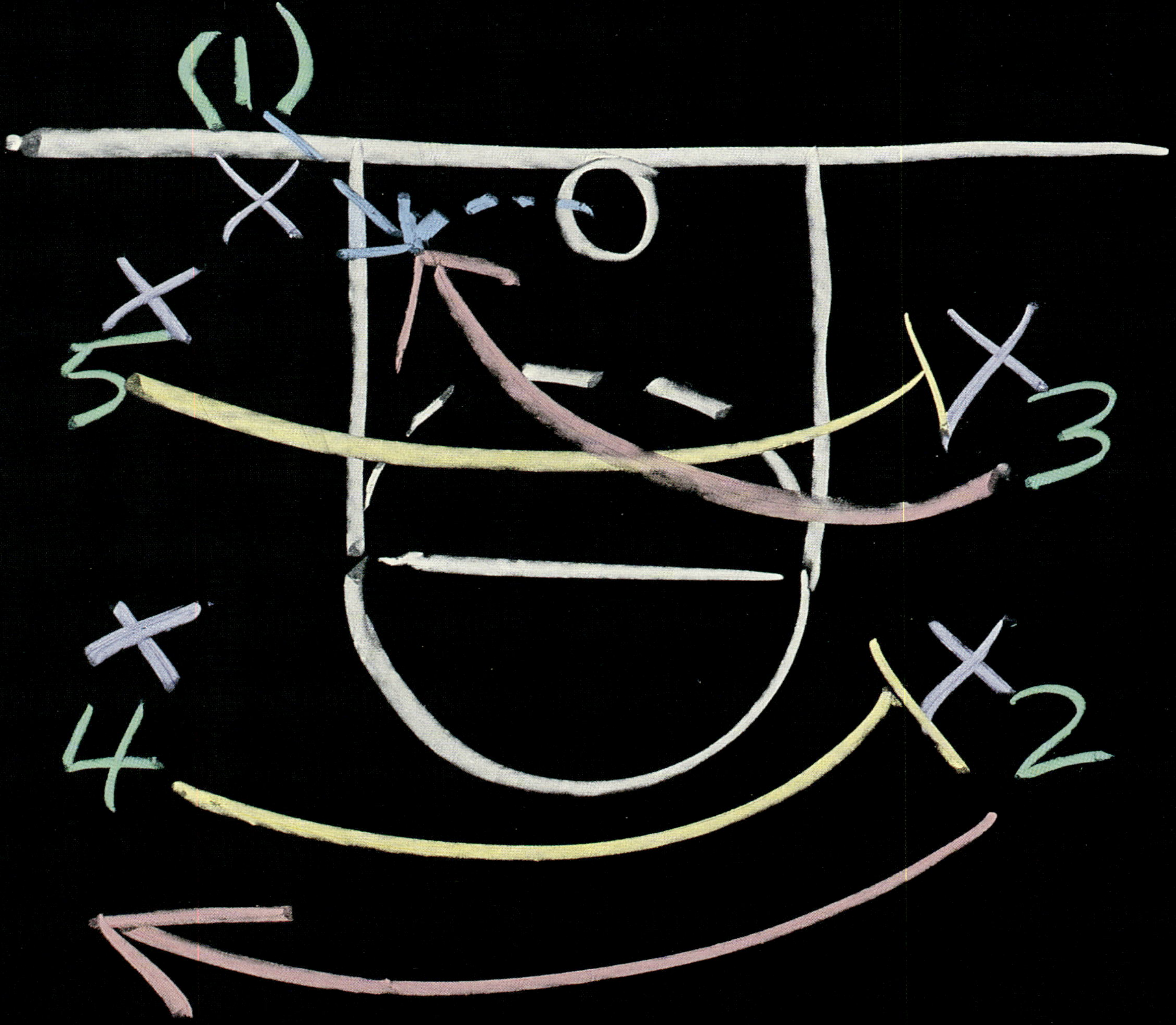

Who are the players? What are their strengths? What are their weaknesses? How do they match-up with your players? These are only a few of the questions that need to be answered before a game plan can be developed.

Who is your target audience? What are you going to say? How are you going to say it? When and where are you going to say it? Do you have a game plan when it comes to developing your company's communications?

We are graphic design and advertising professionals who specialize in creating and implementing your communications game plan. For assistance and inspiration call (303) 296-9909 and ask for the coach.

MULTI
MEDIA
GROUP

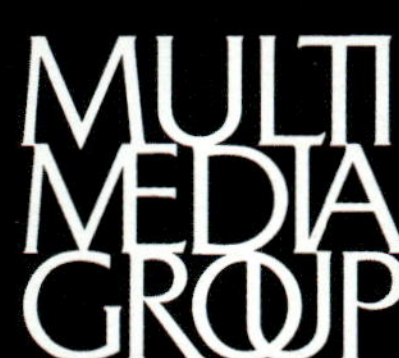

ONE
TABOR
CENTER
Convenient Access to I-25
Preferred 17th Street Address
16th Street Mall Shuttle Access
RTD Terminal Within 2 Blocks
The Shops at Tabor Center
Variety of Restaurants
Picnic Court
The World Class Westin Hotel
On-Site Tabor Athletic Club
Law Library
Underground Parking Garage
State-of-the-art Life Safety Systems
24 Hour Security, 7 Days a Week
For Leasing Information Call:
Trammell Crow Company
1200 Seventeenth, Suite 1900
Denver, Colorado 80202
303/572-6100
TABOR
CENTER

Panorama Park's Most Valued Tenants Office Here Rent-Free

Generations of wildlife have earned their living at Panorama Park and we want to keep it that way. Because people like it when they see a rabbit scuttle across their path, or a family of meadowlarks nesting outside their office window. People also appreciate Panorama Park's unobstructed views of the entire Front Range and convenient access to I-25, I-225 and C-470.

Building sites suitable for almost any concept from 1 to 40 acres, I-25 & Dry Creek Rd. A development of Larrick Corporation. (303) 790-1234

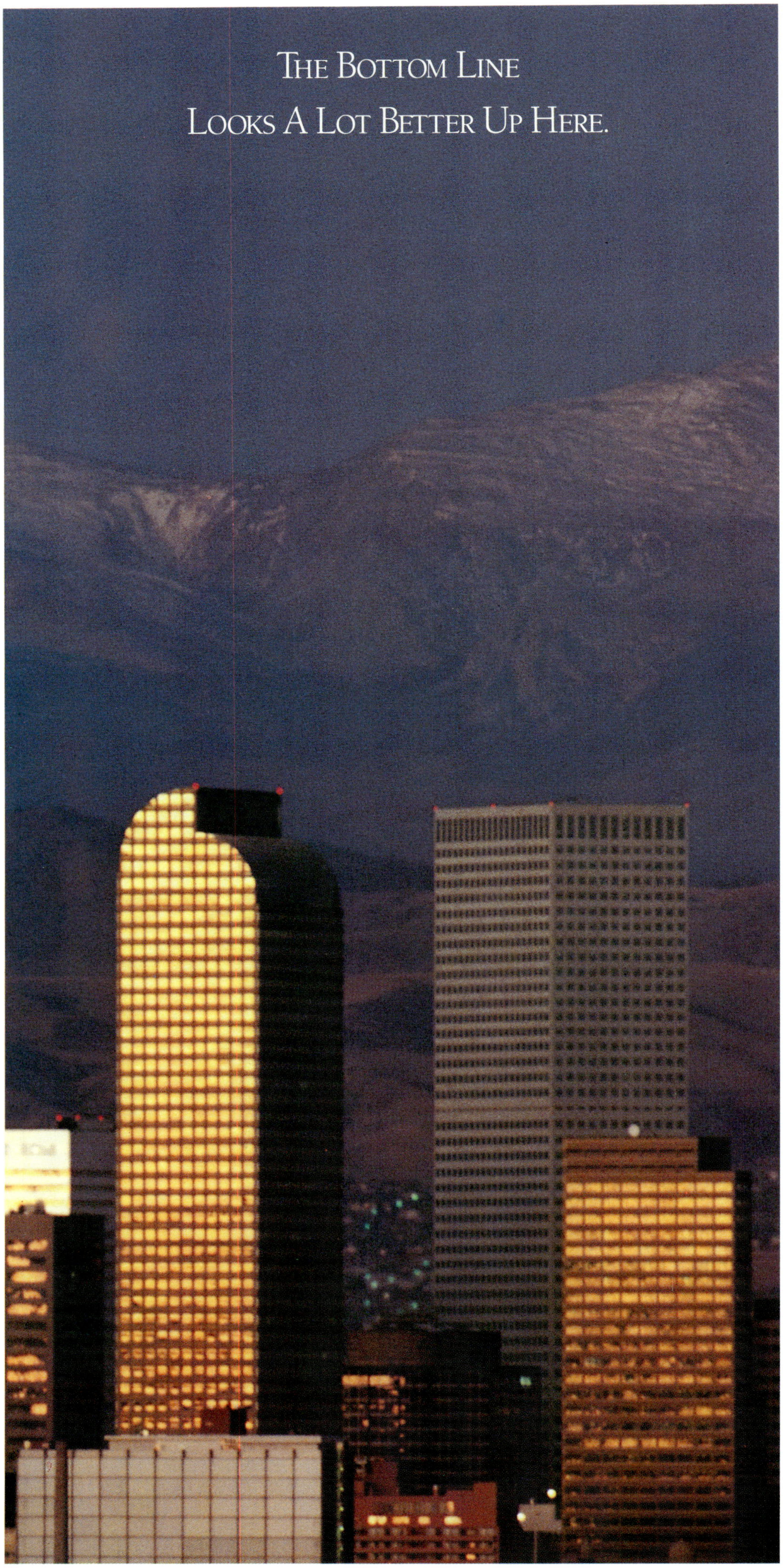
The Bottom Line
Looks A Lot Better Up Here.

Rocky Mountain News columnists Jay Mariotti and Teri Thompson lead an impressive team of writers into this year's Western Regionals.

They'll bring home all the exciting action that has made the NCAA Tournament the premier amateur sporting event of the year.

You'll find Jay and Teri in just the place, the Sports pages of your Rocky Mountain News.

Rocky Mountain News

Denver's Sports Authority

Sunday, March 19, 1989 | Rocky Mountain News | Page 1-S

Sunday Sports

LIFTOUT SECTION

Teri Thompson
Denver Hosts

Jay Mariotti
Relevant, Readable, Remarkable
An insider's view of sports

Denver's Circulation Leader

Rocky Mountain News

Sunday, March 19, 1989 | SUNDAY | SUBSCRIBE 892-NEWS

We Took A Great Idea,

And Reinvented The Carry-On.

Introducing the latest breakthrough rolled out by Samsonite® The Ultravalet™ Carry-On with Wheels — the carry-on that lets you hit the ground running. Thanks to 4 wheels that get the carry-on off your back.

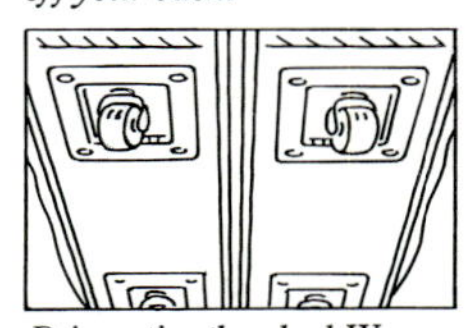

Reinventing the wheel. We recessed all 4 wheels to keep them from getting hung up on objects like your seat. And designed the wheels to keep the bag going where you're going. Not the other way around.

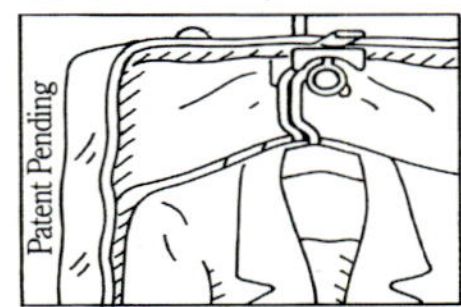

Everything hangs together. Thanks to our special hanging compartment for suits, dresses and coats. And our unique hanger system that locks any type of hanger in place and allows you to pack right from the closet. There's also a strap at the bottom of our extended garment compartment that keeps longer items in place.

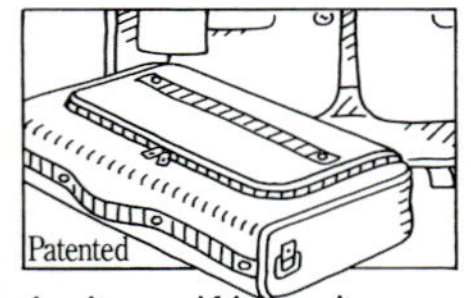

A suitcase within a suitcase. This carry-on is truly unique because of its detachable valet compartment. It can be removed from the main bag and used as a second suitcase, taken out and used as a dresser drawer in your hotel room or left in the bag so that you can live right out of it.

You'll find there are lots of other reasons why people are getting carried away with the Ultravalet Carry-On with Wheels. Like the fact that it actually fits under most airline seats. So hurry on down to a luggage store near you, and you'll see why it's the fastest moving thing on 4 wheels.

Our Strengths Are Legendary.®

GAIN THE COMPETITIVE EDGE

It is the competitive edge that distinguishes winners. It's that extra something that sets you apart from the rest of the field.

Gaining and maintaining that competitive edge requires talent, experience, insight, commitment to quality, an overwhelming desire to be the best, and, above all, teamwork.

Our Denver Touche Ross team of proven professionals will join your team to provide the winning combination of the vast resources of a "Big Eight" accounting and consulting firm with our specialized knowledge of local and regional business climates and requirements.

Gain the Competitive Edge – Call in our team.

Touche Ross

370 Seventeenth Street, Suite 2600
Denver, Colorado 80202-5626
(303) 861-4462

FOR DECADES, WE'VE KEPT OUR EYE ON COLORADO'S TOMORROW.
A forward-looking approach to business is just one reason for our success. And, although our roots reach back through more than a century of Colorado history, it's not our past we focus on.
Because we know past success is no guarantee for the uncertain future. So for us to reach our goals, and help your business do the same, we keep working on ways to make banking with United Bank more efficient, more cost-effective, more flexible, and more useful than banking anywhere else.
Whether it's inventing the region's first intermediate term convertible mortgage or fine-tuning our nationally ranked Cash Management systems, we're not content until we put every bit of our $5.5 billion in resources to the best use for your company.
Forward-moving and forward-thinking. Two reasons why United Bank is ready for whatever your tomorrow may bring.
United Bank
We've got more to give.
Member FDIC

The most exciting line-up off the court.

While you're here for the basketball tournament, be sure to put Village Inn into your game plan. Featured here are some of our star performers, like our luscious Fruit Belgian Waffle, "The Works" Breakfast Skillet, our popular Cross-Country Omelette and our slam-dunk delicious Pancake Sandwich. Pre-game. Half time. Any time. Village Inn serves great food all day long.

Village Inn

28 convenient Metro Denver locations, and 230 nationwide.

JOHN FIELDER'S LATEST BOOK MAKES THIS YEAR'S BEST CORPORATE GIFT!

This year why not give the gift of Colorado to customers, clients, prospects, and friends?

Four years and 2,000 miles of hiking Colorado's most remote natural lands has produced 137 dramatic images by Colorado's favorite photographer, John Fielder. A book that portrays all of Colorado, you witness not only his forays into the wildest regions of the Colorado Rockies, but also the great plains of the east and the plateau country of the western side of the state. From endless fields of wildflowers in the Weminuche Wilderness to sandstone arches and 3,000 foot deep river canyons, you will be astonished by the diversity of the state you thought you knew so well. With a preface by U.S. Senator Tim Wirth.

10″x14″ Exhibit Format • Cloth Bound Hardcover • 137 Full-Color Photographs • Individual Mailing Carton

Quantity discounts are available. Ask Dianne Howie, Director of Corporate Sales, to send you a sample copy today.

Westcliffe Publishers, Inc., 2650 South Zuni Street, Englewood, Colorado 80110,
Phone: 303-935-0900, FAX: 303-935-0903

The Publishers of *Rocky Mountain Basketball — Naismith to Nineteen Ninety*

V O L U N T E E R S

Indian paintbrush garnish the Continental Divide Trail, Weminuche Wilderness Area. Photo courtesy of John Fielder, from Colorado Lost Places and Forgotten Words.

The Denver Organizing Committee thanks the following volunteers who have given their time and energy for the 1990 Denver NCAA Final Four Basketball Tournament.

Brad Anderson
Mary Ashley
Steve Barnett
Dave Belloni
Penny Berg
Christine Bess
Jim Biddle
Callen Borglas
Alan Bossart
Glenn Boychuk
Margie Breeze
Chris Bullard
Jon Burianek
Robert Burrell
Rick Carman
Lauren Casteel
Andy Cladis
Robert Cohen
Mike Contreraz
Barbara Corson
Randy Cronenwett
Tangie Daniels
Elton Davis
John Dee
John Dikeou
Wendy Dotson
Pierre Dubois
Dick Eicher
Ron Elliott
Caroline Fenton
Jody Fiedorowicz
Richard Fleming
Frank Fredericks
Joe Garmatz
Jerry Gart
Rick Gervasini

Jan Anderson
Jim Ayres
Luanne Bastian
Harry Benson
Eric Berger
Kathy Best
David Bird
Tammy Borglas
Dianne Bouller
Buck Boze
Kevin Bromley
Gerry Bullard
Bonnie Burnette
Don Cannalte
Lee Carrothers
Rich Chandler
John Clageti
Tim Colleran
Jack Corn
Jim Corson
Chet Curry
Gary Davenport
Louis Davis
Darrel Delimont
Mike DeSimone
Bruce Downsbrough
Steve Engleman
Greg Elliott
Nora Erickson
Kevin Fenton
Barry Fiore
Tom Fouch
Ken Fulton
Douglas Garrett
John Gart
Greg Gibbs

Laura Anselmo
Terre Barnes
Tom Beckett
Todd Benson
Frank Bernardi
Jerre Biddle
Milt Bollman
Bert Borgmann
Thomas Bowman
Larry Brady
Al Buenning
Rodney Bunting
Richard Burnette
Ken Card
Charles Casteel
Jane Chisholm
Jim Clark
Mark Condon
Bill Corr
Debbie Crapeau
Woody Curtis
Bob Davis
Pat Davis
Phil Demarest
James Donnelly
Deb Dowling
Jerry Eddy
John Elliott
Mercedes Fell
Joe Figlino
Michael Flaherty
Ron Franz
Elaine Gampel
Nancy Garrett
Cindy Gayles
Jack Girtin

Nancy Goebel
Edmundo Gonzales
Cliff Grate
Mike Grose
Kevin Hannon
Dick Harring
Clyde Harris
Karen Hays
Diane Henderson
Rick Hergenreder
Tom Hohensee
Bill Hoople
Janice Hunt
Rodney Hurlbut
Steve Jackson
Tom Jaquet
Rex Jennings
Alan Johnston
Bill Kaufman
Lew Keim
Joyce Kent
Jill Kinney
Jamie Kirchhof
Anne Kleinkopf
Corinne Koehler
Peggy Kopmeyer
Betsy Kropf
Kenneth Landis
Dick Latham
John Lay
Norm Lester
Simon Lipstein
Judy Lotspeich
Craig Mickey
Carolyne Markle
David Martinez
Marilyn May
Thomas McMahon
Murray McNeil
Peter Meersman
David Mejia
DeAnn Metzger
Doug Montgomery
Jerry Nichols
Stephanie Nora
David Ogden
Vicki Peagler
Ernie Peters
Alan Phillips
JoLynne Pierce
Mike Raabe
Steve Raymond
Jim Reese
Bob Rhodes
Rob Rinker
Sal Sanchez
Fred Schaefer
Kathy Scheuerman
Carol Schlueter
Bob Schneebeck
Sharon Schrage
Jarvis Seccombe
Lou Severino
James Shaffer
Gerald Sheridan
Jim Simmons
Joel Smith
Michael S. Smith
Greg Spivak
John Suder
Joe Talty
Ron Taylor
David Thulin
Thomas Urig
Andrea Van Steenhouse
Robert Volzer
Daniel Weikle
Sonja Weiss
Dave Whitney
Marc Williams
Joan Wilson
Don Woodlee
Joseph Yanofsky

Richard Goebel
Bill Goodspeed
Theo Gregory
Leanne Hamlin
Frank Haraway
Teddy Harring
Kate Hastings
Jeff Heider
Ed Henderson
Graham Hill
Noel Hohnstein
Paul Hoskins
Rob Hunt, Jr.
John Hurt
Paul Jacobs
Brad Jeffress
Marvin Johnson
Gary Jomes
Sherry Kauffman
Jim Kelley
Reed Killam
Steve Kinney
Doug Kieswetter
David Kleinkopf
Walt Koelbel
Patrick Kowaleski
John Krueger
Sharon Landis
George Latuda
Gail Lehrmann
Ben Levek
Tim Litherland
Fred Luetzen
Alan Magnuson
Darryl Marks
Ron Mathewson
Kevin McCorry
Mary Beth McKinney
Todd McNeil
Craig Meis
Bob Meldrum
Dianne Mitchell
Tony Navarro
Michele Nichols
Todd Nowek
Doug Otto
Libby Peevy
Joan Peters
Bud Pickford
Ray Plutko
Bruce Rader
John Reddall
Rick Reese
Allen Rice
Elizabeth Rodgers
Steve Saunders
Scott Scheifele
Sharm Scheuerman
Bill Schmausser
Jeff Schofield
Tim Schultz
John Seese
Pat Sexton
Carol Shepard
Lori Sherman
Tim Simmons
Karri Smith
Richard Smith
Taylor Stephens
Larry Sutton
Sharon Tarr
Greg Theophilus
Jan Thulin
Dan Vaaler
Larry Varnell
Bob Warren
Matthew Weiler
Jack Wheeler
Phil Wiland
Joan Wittenwyler
Michael Wolfe
Caroline Writer
Deane Writer
Ed Zorn

Ron Gonzales
Susan Grant
Regis Groff
Margaret Hamlin
June Haraway
Eileen Harrington
Betsy Hayes
Bill Heine
Doug Henninger
Don Hinchey
Ken Holt
Anne Hoskinson
Rob Hunt, Sr.
Carmine Iadarola
Mitchell James
Molly Jenkins
Wendy Johnson
Dick Katte
Howard Kay
Vikki Kelly
Debbie Kinney
Sue Kinney
Michael Klahr
Roger Knight
Maryann Kopelov
George Kresno
Sue Lake
John Laskey
Joe LaVilla
Mary Lester
Peter Liensenfely
Gene Lotspeich
Tom Lyons
Bob Mantooth
Mitchell Martin
Dean May
Lee McCurry
Michael McManus
John McSweeney
Merle Meisner
Ron Merlin
Bill Molitor
Robert Nelson
Steven Nickell
Ann O'Donnell
Tim O'Neil
Jack Painter
Lou Personett
Betty Phillips
Carlos Pierce
Gary Potter
Rebecca Randolph
Kenneth Reed
David Reid
Ron Richards
Marcia Rolander
Elwyn Schaefer
Greg Scheuerman
Keith Schneider
Gene Schnabel
Lynn Schofield
Luann Schwartz
Mel Seigel
John Shaefer
Dottie Sheridan
Chuck Short
Greg Smith
Michael A. Smith
Lynn Sorenson
Jean Stuck
Sharon Sutton
Robert Taylor
David Thistle
Ed Trommeter
Dennis Van Patter
George Vaught
Howard Weese
Gladys Weimar
Leslie Wheeler
Carol Williams
Tom Wittenwyler
Kathleen Wood
Thomas Wynne
Jim Zurcher

Denver Organizing Committee volunteers Chuck Short, Andrea Van Steenhouse and Pat Kowaleski pose with University of Colorado president Gordon Gee.

Joan Wilson, Chairman of Volunteers, above, and volunteers Kathy Scheuerman, below left, with Lynn Schofield at the Tip-off Party for the 1989 West Regional Tournament, Hyatt Regency Hotel. Photos courtesy of Fritz Law.

ACKNOWLEDGEMENTS

Twin peaks of Mount Sopris, aspen and scrub oak enjoy the crisp air of a Colorado autumn day, White River National Forest. Photo courtesy of John Fielder, from Colorado Lost Places and Forgotten Words.

The following individuals and Denver firms contributed to the production of this book.

Denver Organizing Committee Staff:	Roger Kinney, General Chairman; Don Hinchey, Vice Chairman; Caroline Writer, Assistant Treasurer; Tom Foutch, Special Projects
Publisher:	John Fielder, Westcliffe Publishers
Production Manager:	Mary Jo Lawrence, Westcliffe Publishers
Graphic Design:	Tim George, Bruce Iannuzzi, Mark Mulvany, MultiMedia Group
Cover:	Bob Ashe, Ashe/Photography (skyline); Warren Blanc, the Image Maker (player); John Fielder, Western Images (scenic). Also thanks to the Denver Athletic Club, Gart Bros. and model Richard Hayward. Designed by MultiMedia Group.
Contributing Writers:	Bert Borgmann, B.G. Brooks, Irv Brown, Jim Burris, Fred Casotti, Frank Haraway, June Haraway, Don Hinchey, Tom Hohensee, Bud Maloney, Buddy Martin, James B. Meadow, John Mooney, Jim Nantz, John Rayburn, Ken Reed, Kevin Simpson, Larry Varnell, Larry Zimmer
Cartoons:	Drew Litton, *Rocky Mountain News*
Editor:	Bob Diddlebock
Fact Checkers:	Manual Boody, Frank Haraway
Typography:	Max Tyler, Campro Systems, Ltd.
Proofreaders:	Dianne Howie, Pat Quigley
Color Separations:	Bob Schreiner, Capitol Engraving
Printer:	Barry Johnson, Moser Printing
Paper:	J. David Landes, Dixon Paper
Binding:	Bill Hawley, Hawley Bookbinders
Dust Jacket Lamination:	JoAnne Billen, Perma-Graphics inc.
Photo Resources:	Please see each photo for resource.

Bibliography:

Hoose, Phillip M. *Hoosiers, The Fabulous Basketball Life of Indiana*. New York: Vintage Books, A Division of Random House, 1986.

Stern, Robert. *They Were Number One, A History of the NCAA Basketball Tournament*. New York: Leisure Press, 1983.